D0352831

Development & Learning
for Very Young Children

Development & Learning
for Very Young Children

edited by Hilary Fabian & Claire Mould

SAGE

Los Angeles • London • New Delhi • Singapore • Washington DC

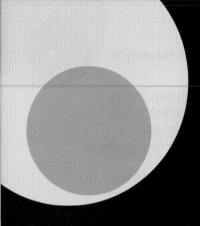

Acknowledgements

We wish to thank the settings where the case studies have taken place – these have provided the 'pictures' of the points that we have made in each chapter and given life to the book.

Key to Icons

Chapter objectives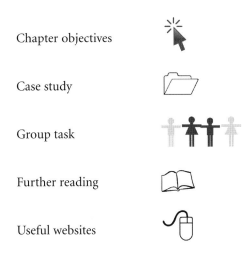

Case study

Group task

Further reading

Useful websites

takes the stance that, in order to really understand how babies and young children develop and grow, it is essential to step back and observe the journeys the children travel throughout their development (Chapter 2). Documenting this learning process provides a narrative from which future experiences can be planned. The more we know about what children do, the closer we come to understanding why they are doing what they do. As we develop this appreciation of babies and young children's behaviour we can endeavour to support and stimulate in a sensitive and appropriate way (Chapter 3).

The second section of the book explores the reality of facilitating meaningful and stimulating practice, that is underpinned by current policy as is necessary (Chapter 4). This involves a discussion examining what constitutes motivating, purposeful learning for young children, clarifying ways in which this can still be achieved while respecting binding policies and procedures. Chapter 5 goes on to outline how a comprehensive awareness and management of legislation and policies need not be arduous and time-consuming and can enable genuine, exciting and relevant experiences. A fundamental part of sustaining and enhancing this effective practice is through the establishment and implementation of practical, accessible self-evaluation tools. The essential role of continual observation and evaluation in developing babies' and young children's learning experiences and the related practicalities are examined in Chapter 6.

The third cluster of chapters focuses on the effective leadership and management of learning environments. Fundamental to this discussion is the consideration of what it is that actually constitutes a successful learning environment and how this can be developed and sustained (Chapter 7). The teams that work within this environment play an integral role in determining the nature of the success, or indeed need for development, of particular learning situations and experiences. In short, effective teams beget effective learning environments. The complexities that contribute to ensuring that the team is appropriately formed and works in a positive way are addressed in Chapter 8. In addition to a sole agency form of provision it cannot be forgotten that by the time children reach 3 years of age they, and their families, have experienced a vast, albeit differing, range of multi-agency support. Increasingly, what were once independent agencies are joining forces (not to mention expertise and experience), with the aim of providing coherent, consistent support. However, the change in dynamics within the environment as a result of this collaboration, and the effect this has on the children in their care, their families and the individual providers needs to be considered. Chapter 9 focuses on the cross-section of individuals who contribute to the child's development and learning, and addresses the reality of managing the union of these contributions to development in a way that is consistent with the children's experience and coherent for these professionals.

The final section concentrates on 'establishing effective relationships'. It begins (Chapter 10) by reinforcing and extending the realities, complexities and importance of interactions between colleagues within a setting. The narrative then broadens to consider other integral relationships that have a direct impact on the lives of babies and young children. The nature of the communications between parents and the providers who work with their child is pivotal to children's emotional well-being and assimilation of development and learning experiences (Chapter 11). If there is little or no genuine dialogue between 'significant others' then there is a risk of mixed or contrasting messages, methods and routines, resulting in the learner feeling confused and alienated. When parents and providers share open, frequent exchanges the learning potential thrives as clear, consistent information is delivered in a sensitive and meaningful way. This section concludes with a focus on the primary importance of ensuring that the relationships that babies and young children experience are positive (Chapter 12). Research tells us that a learner's emotional well-being has a direct bearing on their cognitive learning. If an effective bond is formed between a learner and an educator (whether they be a parent or a provider) founded on knowledge and understanding of interests and needs, then learning will flourish. Where there is a lack of empathy and experiences extend from superficial assumptions, the learning potential will flounder.

SECTION 1
DEVELOPMENT AND LEARNING

SECTION 1

Development and Learning

Child development is seen as the cornerstone to working with children, so we start the book with a look at some of the key theorists and ideas about child development and examples of behaviours. If we consider children's development in Dewey's terms of the social, investigative, constructive and expressive, we can begin to see how our current notions linked to physical, intellectual, emotional and social development match with his ideas (Simpson, 2001). His four 'impulses', developed in the 1890s, demonstrated how children learn by starting from their own interest with each new experience following logically on from the previous experience to help them make sense of their world. In this first section of the book we see how babies and young children learn at their own pace and by following their current interests. We are reminded of the importance of tuning into their way of understanding and level of ability so we can extend these at appropriate times, rather than interrupting the flow of their learning.

The opening chapter begins by outlining what is meant by the term 'holistic development'. It brings together all areas of child development and explores the importance of the holistic development of babies and young children by drawing on the work of Bronfenbrenner, Maslow, Piaget, Vygotsky and others to apply theory to practice and link to the development of government documentation. We visit Bronfenbrenner's mesosystems where children develop in a number of social groupings and are influenced by each; Maslow's hierarchy of need and its relevance to recent government policy; the influence of other cultures and the impact this has on the early years curriculum and subsequent practice; the way that Piaget's stages of development provide milestones; and Vygotsky's influence on social development. These are all put to the test when we are invited to view Harry's development against the Early Years Foundation Stage, Piagetian and Vygotskian perspectives.

The tension between learning stages and phases of education has been diminishing in recent years, to the extent that transition points between phases of education are becoming blurred. Continuous learning, based on the child's individual development and geared towards meeting the individual needs of each child is more common. However, this requires well-qualified adults with knowledge of the way in which children develop, which is drawn from a range of theorists, their own observations and critical evaluation of their own practice.

We move on to look at a particular aspect of development in the early years curriculum, using play as a tool for learning. We sometimes think of the 'subjects' that children learn as being separate – language, creative, physical, mathematical and so on – but Chapter 2 indicates how they link together and, in this instance, language is seen as key to mathematical development. Drawing on play theory, Vygotsky's zone of proximal development, and the use of language, it discusses the use of play in learning to gain an understanding of how babies and toddlers develop mathematically. Their learning is documented using mathematics as a focus as we trace the transitions in their developmental journey from 15 months to 3 years in a series of case studies which demonstrate progression. The chapter enhances the reader's understanding of the importance of play and particularly the use of language in children's learning to develop a shared professional understanding of the diverse nature of different types of play at appropriate stages of development. This underlines the significance of play in development and learning of children from birth and reinforces some of the messages from the first chapter.

Chapter 3 moves away from theory to provide some insights into the behaviours of babies and enhances our understanding of how and why children behave in the way that they do. It highlights, through several examples, the child development theory explored in the first two chapters and puts this into everyday practice. One of the key elements in this chapter is listening and taking note of children's views – even if the children are very tiny babies! This is clearly outlined by the first case study where communicating with the child through listening to their voice and interpreting gestures, provides important aspects to developing relationships.

Understanding normal stages of development for children provides an understanding for expectations of behaviour and helps to develop an awareness of recognizing exceptions to the developmental norm. Some of these are explored in Chapter 1 but we return here to link this again with the need to observe closely so that we have a clear understanding of what the child needs, understand their level of development and respond appropriately to them. By highlighting particular behaviours such as when babies stop crying, readers are encouraged to question their own expectations of children's capabilities at appropriate ages.

Observing, rather than interrupting, play adds to our awareness of the stage of development and gives us an insight into what is needed next. Equally, babies and young children observe adults for feedback and to learn behaviours. Positive feedback, often in the form of non-verbal communication, reinforces the messages that are being exchanged. Consistency in behaviours on the part of the adult is, therefore, a major part of the developing child's learning. Within this chapter the benefits of having a behaviour policy that is consistently upheld by all those working with babies and young children, and is shared with parents, is discussed.

Social development is a central part of this chapter, with examples throughout of the skill that is needed to read nuances in different social situations which, as adults, have taken years to comprehend. Several examples illustrate how children are often sophisticated in their behaviours and in their interpretations of behaviours. The chapter therefore recommends letting children learn how to make friends, join a group and so on, rather than doing it for them, as they have these skills naturally.

Knowing about theories is part of the education of practitioners. We can see from these opening three chapters that child development is complex with many interacting factors as outlined by Oates (2007: 17): 'Genetic and constitutional factors in the child act in constant interplay with caregiving characteristics, with socio-economic circumstances and with child health, such that predicting the precise course of an individual child's developmental trajectory is well-nigh impossible to do with any certainty.'

1

The Holistic Development of Babies and Young Children

Kate Wagner

CHAPTER OBJECTIVES

- To consider a definition of holistic development.
- To think holistically about child development.
- To apply key philosophies to practice.
- To reflect on practice.

What is holistic development?

The word 'holistic' originates from the Greek word 'holos' meaning whole, entire and complete, thus the fundamental interconnectedness of all things (Adams, 1998). Holistic development means looking at the whole child in context and endeavouring to 'find the whole child'.

Every child is unique but at the same time forms identity, meaning and purpose through relationships with family, community, culture and public policies. A child does not experience the world in isolation but develops within the whole society and finds identity within society. Bronfenbrenner (1989: 190) comments that children do not develop 'in a vacuum. We must explore the ecological niche in which the children are living', expressing the view that children are embedded in a series of interacting systems encompassing the multiple influences in children's lives. Holistic development aims to preserve every child's uniqueness while supporting the child in the context of these relationships to ensure each child becomes what Froebel (Froebel Web, 2008) describes as 'all-sidedness, harmony and completeness'. Holistic

Figure 1.1   Influences on the child

development extends beyond the universal normative developmental milestones, which seek to homogenize children, recognizing the importance of all aspects of children's experience. The holistic developmental process could be compared with the nature of a finely balanced gyroscope, spinning, all encompassing, often off kilter, but eventually regaining equilibrium; the spinning wheel is free to take any orientation of external influence. Allowances need to be made for deviations in the stream of development and compensated for in practice. Children should be at the centre of the process (see Figure 1.1).

From the very start of their lives, children are immersed in these influences and become participants in their processes, the most important element of which is the nature of their relationships with the people surrounding them.

Thinking holistically about child development

Holistic development needs to be fostered by adopting a holistic way of thinking about child development. An understanding of the multiple layers of the meanings and experiences of children is the key component in the effectiveness of this approach.

Table 1.1   Frameworks

Every Child Matters **(ECM)**	Birth to Three Matters **(BTM)**
Holistic nature of the five outcomes: • Be healthy • Stay safe • Enjoy and achieve • Make a positive contribution • Achieve economic well-being.	Provides for an holistic 'curriculum framework' for 0–3-year-olds: • Links caring, development and learning • Through the provision of 'joined-up' services
Early Years Foundation Stage **(EYFS)**	Practical Guidance for the EYFS
Combines the holistic ideas and principles underpinning ECM and BTM: • Defines good practice in the early years • Defines early years provision as all experiences provided by early education and care settings	Describes a holistic and logical approach to putting EYFS principles into practice: • How to implement learning, development and welfare requirements of framework • Guidance on progressive, linear child development

---

DISCUSSION POINT

When you are observing a child in your setting, what do you see? In that moment do you see the child as an individual or contextualized beyond the setting? How do you think holistically?

Maslow's hierarchy of human needs (1943) offers a good base from which to start thinking about child development in a holistic way. Maslow suggests that there are five hierarchical levels of need: physiological, safety, social, esteem and self-actualization. An individual must meet the lower-level basic needs before progressing on to the higher-level growth needs. Thinking holistically allows for greater understanding and recognition of what needs have already been met by children and what needs are current and create a gateway for the identification of skills that children will need to develop to allow them to fulfil these needs successfully.

There is broad consensus that early childhood education and care should be delivered holistically and, indeed, in recent years it is claimed that holistic thinking has been the major influence on public policies and strategies (Table 1.1).

These strategies and frameworks have shifted thinking about early childhood education and care from exclusive developmental areas to a holistic arena in which consideration has been given to the type of person society wishes to produce (Russell, 1994). It is useful to reflect on Bertrand Russell's (1994: 28) statement: 'We must have some concept of the kind of person we wish to produce before we can have any definite opinion as to the education which we consider best'. The government's broader aims expressed in *Every Child Matters* (ECM) (Every Child Matters, 2008) are directly linked to the early years curriculum expressed in the themes and principles of the Early Years Foundation Stage (EYFS) (DfES, 2007) through which a child becomes 'a competent learner from birth who can be resilient, capable, confident, and self-assured' with 'positive relationships' in 'enabling environments'. The introduction of a separate early years 'curriculum' has been welcomed by many practitioners as it recognizes the early years as a distinct stage in children's development and education, acting as a catalyst for a holistic way of thinking from birth. Notwithstanding this recognition, the current emphasis on children as individuals expressed in personalized learning interventions threatens to pass over the significance of the broader social and collaborative nature of holistic development and learning.

Many educationalists acknowledge that the potential future lives of children are inextricably linked to early childhood experiences and factors such as emotional well-being, positive identity, a sense of belonging and community which connect children's development (Anning et al., 1994; Bruce, 2004; Katz, 1995). Attachment, self-actualization and lifespan theories can be seen to share a common idealization of the person and consequently, a future quality of life can be framed in the following terms: having a positive attitude towards oneself; establishing positive relationships with others; having a sense of control over one's own actions and environment; having a purpose in life; and, having the opportunity for personal development. Bruce's (2004) idea of a child developing as a 'whole person' embodies this holistic approach to ensure that children perceive themselves as successful learners and live fulfilling lives. Bruner (Shute, 2002) reflected that how children feel about themselves is directly related to the way they learn, and this is central to the connection between development and learning.

DISCUSSION POINT

Do you think that the Birth to Three Matters (BTM) 'curriculum framework' works for or against holistic development? Does it lay the foundations for producing the type of person society wishes to produce?

Historically, holistic thinking has been a central feature of early childhood education and care in other cultures, for example, New Zealand, Finland, and Reggio Emilia, wherein it is apparent that to separate the integral elements of holistic development artificially would deny children the holistic experience (Figure 1.2).

Here it is useful to consider the nature of the early years curriculum in the UK. The Early Years Foundation Stage (DfES, 2007) applies to all pre-school settings and requires that children achieve at school to secure their future personal, social and economic success; prima facie, a holistic way of thinking. From this perspective, the EYFS could be regarded in the form of curriculum as 'product' wherein children are objectified to achieve a particular educational result. According to Spodek (1988: 202), 'what children need to know is determined by what society thinks is important'. Certain knowledge is considered to be more valuable and it is evident that this has always formed the basis of thinking about the early years curriculum.

Te Whariki Early Childhood Curriculum New Zealand	Karvatus Early Childhood Education & Care Finland	Reggio Emilia An Approach to Early Years Education Italy
Holistic Thinking 'To grow up as competent and confident learners and communicators, healthy in mind, body and spirit, secure in their sense of belonging and in the knowledge that they make a valued contribution to society' **Holistic Development – Kotahitanga** • An integrated view of development in which cognitive, social, cultural, physical, emotional and spiritual dimensions of human development are integrally interwoven • The child's whole context, the physical surroundings, the emotional context, relationships with others, and the child's immediate needs at any moment will affect and modify how a particular experience contributes to the child's development • The whole is greater than the sum of its individual experiences	**Holistic Thinking** 'Growing and learning are understood to constitute a life-long process … Early Childhood Education and Care (ECEC) is a … whole comprising the intertwining dimensions of care, education and teaching. These dimensions receive a different emphasis according to the situation, and the age and needs of the child' **Holistic Development** • An integrated whole that ensures consistency and continuity in children's development • Linked to culture and constant change in society • Each child is encountered in accordance with his individual needs, personality, and family culture • Dialogue and partnership between parents and educators	**Holistic Thinking** Learning environments where experiences and methods of teaching, learning, playing and sharing common spaces are interconnected to the point that they become one thing **Holistic Development** • There is no curriculum or guidance. Instead, each year, a new series of related projects are proposed and freely chosen by the children and their teachers • The approach seeks to activate and support children's relationships with other children, family, teachers, society and environment, and all aspects of the surrounding world • The Early Childhood Centre is perceived as a public place for which the community has collective responsibility; 'a place of encounter and dialogue with others'

Figure 1.2 Holistic development in New Zealand, Finland and Reggio Emilia

Sources: Te Whariki (Ministry of Education, 1996); Karvatus (Ministry of Social Affairs and Health, 2003); Reggio Emilia (Rinaldi, 2006).

Indeed, the existence of an early years curriculum demonstrates the shift in thinking about the position and status of children within society. The main discourse which may be expressed as 'academic or developmental' reflects the early education ideologies of romanticism (Rousseau, Froebel), cultural transmission (Skinner, Pavlov) and developmentalism (Piaget), the latter being the most influential in the early years (Spodek, 1988).

The influence of developmentalism in the early years curriculum has created a culture of assessment and testing; in effect, certain knowledge should be learned by a prescribed stage and what is learned represents what is assessed and tested. The consequent pressure that is placed on children to pass tests and assessments means that it is not possible to implement an integrated, child-centred curriculum as emphasis is given to subjects that are tested. As a result, practitioners promote learning outcomes that are directly related to OFSTED judgements at the expense of other learning areas of the curriculum (Smidt, 2002). It is the untested subjects that are often the areas that foster children's enjoyment of learning, personal development and well-being. This begs the question; can the early years curriculum in the UK be defined as holistic thinking?

Much will depend on how the purpose of the curriculum is interpreted. Is it a socializing experience or should it focus on academic development, or is it a mechanism of quality assurance or control?

DISCUSSION POINT

Compare the Early Years Foundation Stage to the New Zealand, Finnish and Reggio Emilia early years curricula. Do you think it is a holistic approach?

From a Marxist perspective, the early years curriculum can be described in terms of power (Giddens, 2006; Haralambos et al., 2004). As knowledge is intrinsic to power, knowledge that can be acquired through school must serve the interests of certain privileged groups, and thus an early years curriculum is designed by members of these groups for their benefit. It is clear that from this perspective the early years curriculum is not a holistic approach, as education is determined by the power struggle, placing restrictions on children in respect of their potential and achievement.

Following Foucauld (McNaughton, 2003; 2005), the early years curriculum forms part of the mechanism for the normalization of society and provides an earlier opportunity for members of society to come under the 'normalizing gaze', particularly when combined with policies in respect of early intervention such as Sure Start, Birth to Three Matters and Every Child Matters. Thus, although early interventions and curricula have the appearance of a holistic approach, Rose (1999: 157) has noted that: 'Childhood is the most intensely governed sector of personal existence', it forms part of a wider plan to normalize children to fit society.

Christie (1997: 134) has commented that the early years curriculum was created in response to 'the need to achieve a degree of social order and economic stability and the need to produce morally responsible subjects, capable of acting in independent, if disciplined ways'. Blenkin and Kelly (1994) perceive the National Curriculum as utilitarian and future-oriented; it is concerned with the product of its aims and objectives, that is, the adult, rather than the child in the present. Its aims and objectives are rooted in current thinking about what is considered to be beneficial for the functioning of society, economy and political systems in terms of achieving 'conformity' (Blenkin and Kelly, 1994: 37). This has been referred to as 'a conforming to society' position whereby it is supposed that the purpose of education is to meet national aims and objectives as defined by government (McNaughton, 2003: 121).

Furthermore, the EYFS is alleged to be a holistic, integrated curriculum. However, it remains divided into distinct curriculum areas:

- Personal, Social and Emotional Development.
- Communication, Language and Literacy.
- Problem Solving, Reasoning and Numeracy.
- Knowledge and Understanding of the World.
- Physical Development.
- Creative Development.

Each area is further subdivided into subjects within the areas of learning, and then set down in terms of Early Learning Goals for each area of learning within a specific age range, and what the practitioner must observe; and what the practitioner needs to do to structure and provide appropriate activities. It is suggested that these divisions provide obstacles to the effectiveness of holistic thinking and practice, and it should be noted that children do not think in divided, linear, hierarchical subjects.

In contrast, Ferre Laevers (2003) has proposed an alternative, process focused approach to the early years curriculum, 'Experiential Education', challenging the dominant means of measuring individual educational outcomes as expressed in systems such as the EYFS. Instead, Laevers (2003) contends that the key to assessing how each child is doing in an early years setting is contained in two dimensions, the child's degree of emotional well-being and the level of involvement. Children are assessed periodically using a list of signals contained in the Leuven Involvement Scale, a five-point scale ranging from Level One, 'extremely low', 'where a child may seem absent and display no energy, activity is simple, repetitive and passive', to Level Five, 'extremely high', 'where a child is concentrated, creative, energetic and persistent with intense activity revealing the greatest involvement' (Laevers, 2003). Accordingly, through this process, practitioners receive instant feedback regarding the quality of their interactions with the children and, consequently, may reflect and take immediate remedial actions.

Applying key philosophies to practice

This section looks at how to apply some of the key philosophies regarding the holistic development of children into practice through a case study of Harry, a 22-month-old boy.

Case Study: Harry

Harry lives with both his parents in a rural area, and spends time not only with his family, but also with his extended family (two sets of grandparents) as well as some time in childcare with a qualified Nursery Nurse, who is also a friend of the family. He has an older brother, Andrew, who is 6 years old and with whom he likes to spend time in play copying his words and actions.

Photo 1   Harry

At 22 months, it would be too soon to predict whether Harry will develop into the type of person that society wishes to produce, based on current government policies and interventions and the early years curriculum that he will be exposed to upon commencing his formal and compulsory education.

First, it is useful to review some of the key philosophies before applying them to Harry's development. From the perspective of developmentally appropriate practice, at 22 months Harry should be meeting the milestones given in Figure 1.3.

Developmental milestones represent what we expect children to be able to do at different stages and they are utilized on the premise that knowledge of what to expect at each stage of children's

Developmental Milestones
18–24 months

- Begin to use up to 40 words (or more) and understand far more words than they can say.

- Enjoy being in the company of other children though they tend to play in parallel rather than with them.

- Have increasing control and can handle a spoon when feeding themselves, or use felt pen to make marks on paper.

- Are now able to walk well and can climb onto a chair.

- Enjoy playing with a range of things including sand, water, foam boards, bricks and telephones.

- May be up and down emotionally as they struggle for independence.

Figure 1.3 Developmental Milestones

Source: Based on DfES (2007).

development facilitates provision of good opportunities to foster development in the best environment. Children are generally assessed by means of observations that are focused on one developmental area. From a Foucauldian perspective, these developmental milestones submit children to the 'normalizing gaze' of the education system through constant hierarchical surveillance and assign their value through normalizing judgements (MacNaughton, 2005).

Drawing on the notion of developmental milestones, behaviourists (for example, Watson, Skinner, Pavlov and Bandura) viewed children's development and learning process as a change in behaviour resulting from stimuli in the external environment that in educational terms could be used to produce behavioural change in the desired direction through reinforcement. Watson (1930: 104) stated: 'Give me a dozen healthy infants, well-formed, and my own specified world to bring them up in and I'll guarantee to take any one at random and train him to become any type of specialist I might select.' However, this empiricist theory is criticized for limiting children's development as it creates a culture of passive learning through which children become unwilling to try new tasks and challenges as they may fail or make errors (Bancroft and Carr, 1999; Flanagan, 2004; Gross, 2002; Hayes, 1994).

According to Piaget, at 22 months, Harry is in the 'preoperational' stage of cognitive development (Figure 1.4).

Piaget asserted that a child is a lone scientist and self-directed in making meaning of the world around himself through schemas and the processes of assimilation, accommodation and equilibration (Bruce, 2004). Piaget suggested that play could assist the learning process by introducing children to new experiences and new opportunities to engage, for example, in symbolic play and games with rules, and is used by children to demonstrate their mastery of a new experience that has been accommodated but not yet assimilated (Bruce, 2004). Through

---

Piaget's Constructivist Stage Theory
Preoperational stage (18 months–7 years)

- Egocentric: unable to understand the world from another's point of view.
- Form ideas from first-hand experiences.
- Cannot understand concrete logic.
- Cannot conserve: unable to understand that quantity does not alter with appearance.
- Uses symbols.
- Role play: increase in play and pretending.

Figure 1.4   Piaget's Constructivist Stage Theory

Source: Based on Piaget (1929).

Piaget's influence, early years practice has been directed towards 'age- and stage-appropriate' activities; 'abstract thought' activities; the use of 'concrete materials to solve abstract problems'; 'first-hand, practical experiences'; 'defining children as "individuals"'; observing children; and providing a prepared learning environment (Daly et al., 2004: 74–5). From a Foucauldian perspective, Piaget's developmental stage theory acts as a normalizing device and the observation of play leads to the monitoring and categorization of children above, below or in line with the developmental norms.

In contrast, in his theory of cognitive development, Vygotsky proposed a holistic, interfunctional approach (Figure 1.5). He contended that children's development and learning must encompass three elements to be effective:

- holistic in nature
- social context
- allow for change and development.

Thus, development is constructed through social interactions with adults and collaborative peers; children would learn from others who had greater knowledge and skills (Riley, 2007). He emphasized the importance of the development of language and pretend play for children to learn about their environment and through which they would be able to experience the zone of proximal development (ZPD) in playing at a level above their capabilities. The ZPD has been described as 'the place where the child and the adult meet' (Palmer and Dolya, 2004: 16) in that the adult provides an important mental support system allowing the child to think in a more complex way. Vygotsky asserted that play creates the ideal opportunity for children to experience a ZPD whereby they can perform beyond their usual age and abilities with the assistance of adults or children who are more knowledgeable than themselves. Gupta and Richardson (1995: 15) offer examples in which children in naturalistic and experimental settings have received a certain level of instruction in order to perform specific tasks in which: 'the teacher's intervention … reduces rapidly with practice' and 'the parental level of control … gradually diminished as it became taken over by the child'. From this apparent operational

---

**Vygotsky's Socio-Constructivist Developmental Theory
Second and Third Years of Life**

- Child–adult joint object-centred action.

- Children in need of adult help as social meanings cannot be discovered independently.

- Mastery of the way to use social objects.

- Creation of the zone of proximal development.

- Adults accepted as mediators of this activity.

- Children imitate adult actions with objects and toys in accordance with their social meanings.

- Children have mastered the gestural means of object-centred communication with adults and, therefore,

- Fast acquisition of new language as:

    - they need new means of communication with adults
    - internal tool of self-regulation
    - development of symbolic thought.

Figure 1.5   Vygotsky's Socio-Constructivist Developmental theory

Source: Based on Karpov (2005).

structuring, it is suggested that play may be enhanced through the interventions of significant others as 'play contains all developmental tendencies in a condensed form' (Jones, 2004: 196).

Observations of Harry have been made using a holistic way of thinking, resulting in an eclectic approach making reference to useful key philosophies; examples follow.

Harry appears to be a happy and cheerful child. He shows good attachment to his family and extended family, and displays secure attachment when he has spent time apart from his primary carer, his mother. He displays a need to interact with others and spend time talking, playing, and engaging with others. Within the EYFS (2007: 31) statements about expected developments in Personal, Social and Emotional Development in the age range 22–36 months, a child should be learning 'social skills, and enjoy being with and talking to adults and other children'. Harry has demonstrated that he fulfils this developmental requirement.

In playing with two other children, Emily (23 months) and Helen (29 months), Harry appears to be the dominant influence; Helen exhibits passive behaviour in respect of this, while Emily challenges it. In Piagetian terms, Harry appears to be able to assimilate and accommodate his past experiences, providing him with a way of thinking about, and dealing with, Emily's confrontational behaviour (perhaps because of his interactions with his older brother, Andrew) in a manner that displays an ability to respond to the feelings and wishes of others (DfES, 2007: 31) and will often incorporate her game into his. From a Vygotskian perspective, Harry could be said to have learned to deal with confrontational behaviour and to negotiate a situation with other children from observing models in his environment and imitating this behaviour. In contrast, Emily's confrontational behaviour may be interpreted in Piagetian terms as a schema she has constructed in which she deals with expressing her ideas and play through physical challenges to others. Vygotskian theory could also be used to argue that Emily's behaviour is modelled. Hannah displays more passive characteristics than the other two children and again this behaviour could be interpreted in Piagetian and Vygotskian terms.

Harry's capacity for language and his vocabulary have been limited; he had been relying on a number of key words, expressions and gestures to communicate with others – no, yes, Mummy, Daddy, Nana, Grandad, please, OK, o-oh, see, here, there, up, good. At about 20 months, he experienced a language explosion. Within the EYFS (DfES, 2007: 42–3) statements for expected developments in Communication, Language and Literacy, between 16 and 26 months, children should be able to 'Use single word and two-word utterances to convey simple and more complex messages' and 'Understand simple sentences'; between 22 and 36 months, a child should be able to 'Learn new words very rapidly and are able to use them in communicating about matters which interest them'. Harry likes to play with trains with his older brother, Andrew. From about 15 months, Harry referred to all the trains as 'Choo-choos'. His older brother referred to the trains by their names (for example, Thomas, Edward, James, Percy, and so on) and created stories about the trains for Harry using the correct vocabulary (for example, rails, station, Fat Controller, bridge, points, and so on) which he acted out, with Harry imitating his actions. Now Harry acts out his own stories with the trains and builds tracks, and lines up and connects the trains and carriages in long rows; he knows all the names of the trains and is able to construct more complex sentences using the correct vocabulary. From a Vygotskian perspective, Harry has not only rapidly acquired language in a short period of time but has also developed abstract thought in his ability to attribute specific names to the trains and act out with them in character (for example, Diesel 10 is bad, Thomas is good, the Fat Controller is in charge). This development could be attributed to the creation of a zone of proximal development between Harry and his older brother, and others who play this game with him. In Piagetian terms, it can be observed that Harry has an existing connection schema. Harry has been able to assimilate and accommodate this existing connection schema and has altered it to incorporate acting out his stories as a result of the interaction with his brother.

Harry was observed using pencils and paper to draw. Harry's use of fine motor skills to use and manipulate the drawing equipment (pencils and paper) is well developed and he expresses enjoyment at mark-making and creating pictures which he then wishes to show and tell and experience praise and reward. If he does not like a pencil or drawing he throws it away, manifesting his emotions through physical gesture. Within the EYSF (DfES, 2007: 102) statements for expected developments in physical development in the age group 22–36 months, Harry exhibited well-developed fine-motor skills within the normal developmental limits for his age range in showing 'increasing control in holding and using … mark making tools'.

These are just a few examples of how Harry's development may be interpreted. All children develop individually and at different rates but in broadly similar sequences. Harry's development represents just one example of this developmental process. Children grow and learn in their own way, for example, Harry's friends, Emily and Helen, may have reached different developmental stages to one another and to Harry. As mentioned earlier, the artificial divisions of the EYFS do not represent a holistic approach and practitioners should remember that each area has the capacity to be cross-referenced with the other areas to provide a more holistic picture of children's development.

GROUP TASK

- Make individual observations of children in your setting.
- Explain to the group what you observed.
- Apply key philosophies together to provide an evaluation of the children's development and make recommendations for their development.

In addition, practitioners should be aware of the hidden agenda in their own practice. As Devereux (1997: 77) has commented: 'Observation raises our awareness of our own beliefs and values, and encourages us to be more conscious of how these affect the interpretation of what we see.'

Reflecting on practice

Research has shown that the critical component in early childhood education and care is the education of the adult, as it is recognized that children's learning outcomes are consequent upon the effective role of the adult (Erikson Institute, 2008). Knowledge of child development theories is one of the most important components of professional practice as it enables practitioners not only to identify developmental behaviours and stages in children but also to understand the complex and interwoven nature of the components involved in their holistic development (EPPE, 2003; Katz, 1997).

Practitioners should develop a personal theory of holistic development in practice, drawing on various aspects of the pioneers/theorists rather than relying on a single theory. Current educational practices are informed by many child development theories because individually they are insufficient in creating a comprehensive understanding of the child. In addition, this personal theory should be informed by practitioners' observational experiences, coupled with an awareness of personal values and judgements. It is clear that the essence of good practice is to critically evaluate how and why we practise in a certain way; consider who benefits from our practice; who is disadvantaged by our practice; and how we can improve our understanding in context.

> ### DISCUSSION POINT
>
> Which key theories do you use in your practice? Consider why, how and when you use them. Are they beneficial to your practice? Which key theorists influence your co-workers' practice?

Reflecting on your own approaches to teaching and learning provides a greater understanding of the relationships between planning, acting and evaluating. It is essential to reflect on personal philosophy and goals, and to question personal reasons for adopting specific perspectives. The approaches adopted by other practitioners should be considered and should inform your own practice in order to benefit from a greater understanding of the role of the practitioner. In addition, it is useful to consider comparative curricula, for example, in New Zealand, Finland and Reggio Emilia (see page 13) to develop holistic thinking about the early years curriculum.

If a practitioner is reflective in practice, a theoretical knowledge together with information gathered from observations should form a good foundation for the development of a personal holistic theory for practice. Practitioners need to give value to the notion of the holistic development of children to support and extend children's opportunities and experiences in a knowledgeable way, not only taking into account child development theory and current policy, but also engaging in critical reflection of their understandings and practice.

Further reading

Piaget, J. (1929) *The Child's Conception of the World*. London: Routledge and Kegan Paul.
Russell, B. (1994) *On Education, Especially in Early Childhood*. London: Routledge.
Vygotsky, L. (1986) *Thought and Language*. 2nd revd edn. Cambridge, MA: MIT Press.

Useful websites

The Early Years Foundation Stage, DCSF (2008) www.standards.dcsf.gov.uk

Effective Early Learning Project, Teaching Expertise (2008) www.teachingexpertise.com

2

Understanding How Babies Develop and Learn Through Documenting Their Learning Journeys

Jane Bulkeley

CHAPTER OBJECTIVES

- To understand progression within a specific area of learning.
- To consider the sequence of mathematical abstraction and how number awareness develops.
- To explore how play and talk contribute to learning about number.

The Early Years Foundation Stage Framework (DfES, 2007a) makes it clear that a balanced and integrated approach to all areas of learning and development to facilitate progression is fundamental to effective practice. The value of such an approach is well established with Moyles (1994; 2005) and Drake (2005) discussing the benefits of giving attention to the all-round development of the whole child. In spite of this, it remains essential that practitioners understand how development within a specific area of learning occurs. Thus, while learning is holistic, the following chapter focuses on the learning journey of a young child's mathematical development, looking at the progression along the spectrum of mathematical understanding with particular emphasis on numbers for counting and as labels.

There are three fields of mathematical experience, each with its own characteristics with which children must become familiar. These are space, number and quantity, each of which is not entirely separate from the others. Numbers are used in a world of space and can tell us something about its properties. Without number we cannot measure quantity, as we need to be able to count the measuring units applied. In the adult world mathematics is an abstract concept, however, the key to understanding and learning about number can perhaps be found in the natural capacity for learning about their physical surroundings and environment for even the youngest of children.

The sequence of mathematical abstraction

As children's thought processes are significantly less sophisticated than those of adults, by following the natural biological sequence and pattern of human growth it is clear that advanced forms of communication such as the written word are inappropriate in the earliest stages of a child's learning journey. Instead, secure foundations must be laid utilizing both concrete resources and first-hand experiences. Instinctively, babies see, feel and explore physical things. They gradually come to know and understand that physical things can be represented by a name. Later, they will recognize pictures of those things and later still will associate them with written symbols. All their experiences, including mathematical experiences, will follow this sequence of abstraction which can be categorized as follows:

E – experience with physical objects
L – (spoken) language that describes the experience
P – pictures that represent the experience and
S – (written) symbols that generalize the experience (Liebeck, 1984: 16).

However, the transition across this sequence of abstraction cannot be achieved unless children:

- have physical (first-hand) experience of number
- acquire and apply language skills to support their understanding of what number is and how it works.

In the early years it is therefore essential that young children have the opportunity to touch number in the sense of being able to manipulate groups of objects and to use the language associated with it to enable them to comprehend its realness and applicability as a tool for life. This is achieved through both their day-to-day lived experience and the artificial learning environments in which they are placed.

The development of number awareness in young children

To be effective, such learning environments should reflect a child's interests and meet their needs, physically and cognitively. Munn (1997) argues that young children count less from an awareness of number and its intrinsic usefulness in life and more as imitators of observed actions. Children therefore need to be stimulated 'to develop their own numerical goals, as quantitative counting is not often part of their behavioural repertoire' (Thompson, 1997: 1). Munn (1997) describes three phases of developing number awareness in pre-school age children: first, a number word sequence is learnt through frequent repetition of a set of words in a predetermined order. Alongside this, children will also learn 'the appropriate contexts for counting'. Later, counting becomes an activity as children start to 'coordinate pointing, objects and number words'. Finally, children will 'integrate counting and cardinality' using their knowledge of number to answer questions about how many and label 'sets' (Munn, 1997: 11). Such progression depends on children acquiring and becoming increasingly sophisticated in the application of their physical, verbal and thinking skills (Munn, 1997). This in turn depends on the opportunities and experiences in working with number offered to them. It is the role of the practitioner to guide and support a child through a journey of discovery so that a successful transition from dependence on physical objects to using symbols can be achieved. There are two key elements to this: an active approach, through play, and talk.

Play and talk as tools for learning

Traditionally the early years curriculum has centred on play and talk as tools for learning, however 'play' and 'talk' need to be purposeful, relevant and challenging (Bennett et al., 1997; DES, 1990) for learning to occur. Structured opportunities for active experience with physical objects, the language associated with them and to link the physical, verbal, pictorial (books/stories) and abstract (labels) represent the process by which young children are helped to make sense of their learning and the world around them (DES, 1990; DfES, 2007b). Gopnik et al. (1999) state the same mechanisms that drive children to make sense of their world also drive them to pay attention to what they hear and to learn how to apply that knowledge and use associated language themselves.

The Plowden Report (DES, 1967) described play as the 'principal means of learning in early childhood'. Although the value and role of play has been the subject of much debate through many decades, it is attributed with being essential to development as an 'educationally powerful process' (Wood and Bennett, 1997: 22) that continues to underpin quality early years curricula. In recent years it has been taken increasingly 'seriously by policy-makers' (Wood and Attfield, 2005: 1). This is reflected in the Early Years Foundation Stage practice guidance which states that 'play underpins the delivery of all the EYFS ... indoors and outdoors' and 'all development and learning for young children' (DfES, 2007b: 7).

Despite this recognition of its worth, there is no agreed definition of play, instead it is seen as having many distinguishable forms, for example, role play, constructive, imaginative and free-flow (Wood and Attfield, 2005). It is not possible within the confines of this chapter to examine play and its worth as an educational tool in the early years, however, some attention is given to explaining its role in engaging children in the process of learning. Play makes an important and holistic contribution to the 'three domains of development – cognitive, affective and psychomotor' (Wood and Attfield, 2005: 119) and can be used as a means of supporting a particular area of learning without segregating it from the curriculum as a whole. Utilizing the properties and characteristics of play as a tool for learning is therefore both meaningful and relevant to a child and constitutes a solid base platform from which practitioners can introduce increasingly complex concepts to develop knowledge, skills and promote progression (DfES, 2007b; Wood and Attfield, 2005).

Language is a powerful tool and asset (De Boo, 2000; Vygotsky, 1986, in Brown, 1998: 75). Its development is essential to lay the best foundations for later learning (Andreski and Nicholls, 1999). Bruce (2004) described children as investigators of language who experiment with it to learn how it works. Developing and using appropriate language establishes patterns of behaviour across the curriculum to assist all-round development and progress, including mathematical understanding (Bearne, 1998). Establishing an environment where all learners can be included in 'talk' is identified as good practice by the DfES (2002). However, this environment needs to be one with which children can identify, where they are encouraged to actively explore and investigate concepts physically and verbally for themselves (Wood and Attfield, 2005). Play is a situation which is rich with language possibilities. While play is the door which opens a world of opportunities to the child, language holds the key.

DISCUSSION POINT

Does the environment in which we work offer opportunities for play and talk? How do we balance the child's need to be creative and manage their own play with ensuring progression in learning and development?

The starting point for supporting and planning for children's development is where a child is (Drake, 2005) in relation to what they 'know, understand and can do' (Rodger, 2003: 34). To progress, children need to be challenged, shown and guided. Bruner and Vygotsky both saw the benefit of children learning in partnership with a more experienced companion to support or extend their grasp of a concept and move forwards in their learning, focusing on 'the role of communication and structured intervention' (Bartlett and Burton, 2007: 126). This relates to what children can do, how they do it and the reciprocal exchange of vocabulary in the process.

GROUP TASK

Can you think of a time when you took the role of a 'more experienced other'? What did you do to extend the child's thinking? Was this effective? Can you identify why this was?

Vygotsky's theory of learning depends on a social model through the involvement of a more knowledgeable party which provides a forum for learning to be social and supported and from which adults withdraw from time to time, returning to maintain contact and confidence. The use of language as a tool is integral to the development of mathematical thinking and the presence (transient or otherwise) of an adult (or peer) who can model more sophisticated language through reciprocal 'shared conversations and joint activity' increases the effectiveness of experience (Wood and Attfield, 2005: 99). While young infants are thought to have an intrinsic capacity to discriminate some mathematical concepts, such as more and less, the language associated with this develops later as part of an independent process (Xu and Spelke, 2000). The technical language of a subject must therefore be experienced through opportunities that are both spontaneous but sometimes structured and therefore, contrived.

This social model relates well to Munn's (1997) first steps in using numbers for counting, that is, the acquisition of knowledge of number names and their correct order. Until this 'sequence' of number is learned, children cannot begin to count objects and attribute meaning to number. In this context, the use of stories, songs and rhymes by practitioners to promote relevant language acquisition is an essential feature of good early years practice with children aged between approximately 8 and 20 months (DfES, 2007b). It is at this stage of development that children begin to develop an awareness of number names through their enjoyment of action rhymes and songs. Opportunities must be sought, made and taken to model the vocabulary of counting from 0 to 5, 0 to 10 and beyond both verbally and by making links with physical objects, whether fingers, puppets, children or other objects. Opportunities to demonstrate the physicality of number and its application in the world around us should always be taken. This indicates a purpose to number in life which increases its validity as a worthwhile pursuit (Rodger, 2003).

Case Study: Numbers for labels and for counting

A small group of children aged about 15–18 months are seated on large cushions on the floor with an adult engaged in counting rhymes, stories and songs. The adult sings 'Round and round the garden like a teddy bear' with each child in turn. Next they sing 'Five little teddy bears jumping up and down' and then move on to reading *One Little Teddy Bear*, a lift-the-flap book. The adult models the counting and encourages the children to join in. When singing, the adult shows her hand with the appropriate number of finger puppets as the song progresses. She encourages the children to join in with the actions. Such short sessions provide regular opportunities for children to practise counting in a safe and fun environment. In this way they became familiar with number order and gained confidence to join in. Number skills can then be applied by introducing numbers at snack time and when using resources by counting children and then the snacks, drinks or equipment and encouraging the children to count along or independently.

It is during the years before school that 'children learn number words, begin to relate number language to their existing number sense, as well as develop an appreciation of the ways that these number words can be used for counting' (Fuson, 1988, in Aubrey, 1997: 21). Thus, possession of the language of counting is the first phase of the transition of mathematical understanding and is continued by rooting activities in the child's world. This continuum of learning experience is achieved through the use of play and familiar resources that allow children to recognize and build on previously learned concepts. This not only provides opportunities to repeat experiments but also offers the security that familiarity brings which impacts on emotional well-being and thus confidence.

This example has some similarities with Floyd's (1981) 'do, talk and record' model. The learning cycle starts with the child doing and talking alongside the adult, followed by tasks when the child has an opportunity to do and talk in small peer groups and to record and check, with a final record being made that will be both public and accessible. This model particularly emphasizes the need for using mathematical language and the repetitive use of it. Further, while the opportunity for peer collaboration and talk alongside the adult makes a significant contribution to progress, small-group work like this also provides observational and assessment opportunities for the practitioner with issues that arise with large groups (DfES, 2002).

Again, access to these resources should be freely available through continuous provision to allow the children to revisit the ideas and concepts presented to reinforce their experience and understanding. Time to explore resources creatively is fundamental to securing progression through the sequence of abstraction. Children need to try out ideas for themselves. They must identify with the concept to be mastered and understand its relevance and purpose for them. A child's spontaneous interactions with their environment and resources (physical and human) provide a window for observation and assessment that allows the adult to intervene strategically to deepen and extend thinking, and thereby aid progression.

GROUP TASK

Observe children using resources from continuous provision. Consider the following:

- Who accessed the resources? Did they work alone or collaboratively?
- How were the resources used?
- What vocabulary was used?
- Did they ask and answer questions? If so, what?
- Was this the same as or different to the way the resources had been introduced? Discuss this.
- Did an adult intervene? If so, for what purpose and was this achieved?

This chapter has considered how young children learn about numbers for counting, and as labels, as a focused example of the progression through the sequence of mathematical abstraction. It suggested that children should be immersed in a language and vocabulary-rich environment rooted in 'doing', beginning with number songs and rhymes and progressing to manipulating objects to aid counting for a purpose in an increasingly abstract form.

The transition across the spectrum of mathematical understanding requires progressing from the concrete physical experiences of the instinctive explorations of the youngest children, to using abstract symbols. Children therefore need opportunities to touch, manipulate and feel what number is and to demonstrate through practical and verbal examples what it means when applied in everyday situations. This is facilitated by providing opportunities for purposeful play and talk. Play allows children to investigate new and quite sophisticated ideas, with the practitioner supporting (Griffiths, 2005) through encouraging and promoting discussion and demonstrating appropriate vocabulary.

'Maths and play are very useful partners' (Griffiths, 2005: 184); however, we should not underestimate the role of language in mathematical development. Effective progression in number lies in opportunities to explore number physically and verbally in a context that children can relate to and in which they can flourish.

DISCUSSION POINT

How will this lead into the next stage of development? For example, using number names more accurately in play. How would you support this?

Further reading

Broadhead, P. (ed.) (1995) *Researching the Early Years Continuum.* Clevedon: Multilingual Matters.
Penn, H. (2005) *Understanding Early Childhood: Issues and Controversies.* Maidenhead: Open University Press.

Useful websites

www.everychildmatters.gov.uk

www.standards.dcsf.gov.uk

3

Developing an Appreciation of Babies' and Young Children's Behaviour – Why Do They Do What They Do?

Frances Morton

CHAPTER OBJECTIVES

This chapter discusses:

- Babies' and young children's sophisticated communication abilities.
- Effective communication being dependent upon sending and receiving messages in a known social context.
- Proficiency in how we interpret, and respond to, a baby's signals affecting their development and future behaviour.
- Allowing young children opportunities for taking control.

Behaviour is the result of interaction with others and the environment and relies on effective communication to be socially acceptable. Interpreting the messages between baby and carer is fundamental to the developing relationship and, since both baby and carer are new to the relationship, they have to learn from each other. But as well as learning from the children in our care we need to remind ourselves to enjoy their company and share their obvious pleasure in their growing accomplishments.

Case Study

Grace, a 6-week-old baby, was being bottle-fed by Zara, an adult. After a while Grace turned her head away and Zara continued to try and feed her. Grace turned her head away again and gave a little cry. Zara tried again to encourage Grace to take more feed, but Grace turned her head away from the teat again, cried and arched her back. Zara persisted in trying to encourage Grace to take more feed, but Grace continued to cry. As Zara persisted Grace's cries increased and she closed her eyes, turned her head away and squirmed in Zara's arms. Zara jiggled her up and down and Grace's cries decreased and with her eyes still closed she accepted the teat in her mouth, sucked on it a couple of times and then fell into a shallow sleep. Zara moved the bottle away from Grace's mouth and, holding her more upright, she gently patted her back to encourage the release of any trapped air in Grace's stomach. Grace opened her eyes briefly then closed them again.

Grace was able to indicate that she had had sufficient milk and did not want any more. She first showed this when she turned her head away. As Zara persisted in offering her more milk Grace indicated her desire to stop more strongly, by crying. When Zara continued to offer her milk Grace closed her eyes to cut out further stimulation. Eventually when all other endeavours failed she fell into a shallow sleep. Young babies will demonstrate this early communication capability to show when they do not want a stimulus to continue. The nature of the stimulus may be physical, emotional, social or cognitive and their cue to stop may be misinterpreted by a carer who unintentionally responds in direct opposition, trying to increase the stimulation in response to the baby's cry. Usually, however, a baby gets their message across and the carer will stop whatever they are doing, try something else and may lay the baby down for a rest.

During the first few weeks parents and carers can only guess why a baby is behaving in a particular way until the baby develops more focused expressions and they have more cues to help them guess fairly accurately what the baby is signalling. The most well-known behaviour is crying with the most common cause being hunger. But babies may cry if they are feeling uncomfortable in some other way, such as in pain, or suffering from extremes of temperature. Very young babies appear to like quite warm ambient temperatures, warmer than most adults find comfortable. With many places being centrally heated nowadays a baby may get too hot during the day but they are more likely to feel too cold at night. Most young babies cry when they are undressed, in particular when the item next to their skin is removed. They will cry even if they are warm and it is probably more the feeling of exposure that upsets them. Some babies may cry if they have a dirty or wet nappy, but this is unusual and more commonly it is the comfort from contact with their carer or even from a change in position that stops their crying rather than the clean nappy. However, it is important to remember that keeping a baby clean and dry is part of providing for their well-being, showing them respect and helping them develop self-respect.

Sometimes a baby will cry and there appears to be no specific reason and this can be upsetting for their parents or main carers as they try one thing after another in an attempt to discover the baby's needs. One of the most distressing of these occasions is when the baby suffers from what is commonly regarded as colic. In the past this was considered to be a digestive problem, possibly trapped air in the digestive tract, but it is still not clear why babies scream in this distressing way, drawing up their knees and giving all indication of being in acute pain. These spasmodic attacks usually occur after the evening feed and the baby can only be pacified momentarily before screaming again. This distressing behaviour is usually over by the time a baby reaches 3–4 months. Overstimulation is a less well-known reason for a baby's cry, and from a very early age a baby can indicate when they wish to stop an activity, as Grace did to show she had finished feeding. But it is generally more difficult to detect when young children are overstimulated than understimulated. Attending group sessions at too young an age, for example, can be over stimulating for young infants with too much confusion of noise and activity.

GROUP TASK

- Look closely at your work environment. Is it designed more for stimulation or relaxation? Does everything serve a purpose? Is there anything you would change?
- Observe young children in play situations to detect any signs of overstimulation. Pay particular attention to the environment and the interactions. Exchange your experiences with colleagues who have observed different age groups to cover the age ranges of 0–3 months, 3–9 months, 9–12 months, 1–2 years and 2–3 years.

DISCUSSION POINT

Should environments be designed especially for young children? Do we have the same standards of quality in environments for children as we do for adults? Is this important?

Human infants are born with a drive to learn and their behaviour is a manifestation of this intrinsic motivation as they strive to discover and understand the world around them. We want to understand this behaviour so that we can support their development. To do this we need to learn from them as well as expecting them to learn from us. We are more experienced communicators and so we are in a better position to interpret their cues and respond accordingly, but it is easier for us to consider the world through the adult mind, as opposed to the child's, because they use speech to communicate, and we can make educated guesses since we have more recent personal experience from an adult perspective. Nevertheless, even if the person is articulate it does not necessarily mean they can tell us what they were really thinking, or that we can comprehend their behaviour in relation to their thoughts, as we all have our own reality of the world. We can all relate incidents when we have been misunderstood ourselves or when we have misinterpreted the thoughts of others. If it is this difficult to understand why adults behave in the way that they do, we can appreciate the difficulties of effective communication between baby and carer when both are learning a new system. The only way to become competent in the system is to observe, practise and act on feedback received.

Babies and children learn by observing us, practising their new skill and adapting their behaviour in accordance with the feedback they receive from others and their environment. In turn we also observe the children in our care and use this not only to discover their interests and to be familiar with their capabilities but to help us understand the individual child and why they behave in particular ways. When we watch babies play we take a lot of their behaviour for granted and just accept that is what babies do. But if we consider the significance of their actions we can appreciate why they behave in the way they do and we are in a better position to respond appropriately to provide positive and satisfying learning experiences. Although there are cultural differences in how we respond to babies' cries, a general worldwide basic pattern of comfort is, first, we talk to them, then we touch them and then we pick them up. A baby learns that when they cry someone responds. The more synchronized the interactions between the carer and the baby, the more a positive relationship is formed. If a baby's cue for initiating play is interpreted accurately and the carer plays with the baby until they correctly interpret another cue from the baby indicating they wish to stop the activity, then the carer and baby are synchronized in their interactions.

Just as communication does not depend totally on the spoken language, a baby does not rely only on crying to communicate. We use parts of our body to express our feelings and although much of this is conveyed through facial expressions, such as an upward-turned mouth in smiling to show happiness or downward-turned mouth in pouting to show unhappiness, our moods can be interpreted from other body gestures. Some of this we learn by copying the behaviour of others and some we develop as unconscious expressions of our feelings, such as holding our body in a state of tension through muscle tone if we are under stress. Through watching others we observe the different behaviour and learn to interpret the signs of body language. Again, some of this we acquire consciously and some unconsciously; for example, in a crowded street we rarely bump into another person because we send out and receive signals of our intended movements, but we are unaware that we do this. When we do collide with someone it is usually because we have been distracted and not sent or received an appropriate signal, or for some reason after sending an unconscious signal of our intended line of travel we suddenly change direction, such as when we stop to look at something which has caught our eye, or see someone we know. Newborn babies show a preference for human faces to other sights, and they are capable of copying a simple facial movement such as sticking out the tongue from the mouth if they are held in a common nursing position, so that their face is approximately 20 to 30 centimetres away from another person's face. This is sophisticated behaviour for someone who has never seen a face before, and certainly not seen their own face and will probably not do so for a number of weeks. When we consider speech and gesture as two main elements of communication, we can appreciate the significance of crying and a baby's ability to copy facial expressions as the earliest signs of a baby's communication capability, and these can be expressed within minutes of birth.

GROUP TASK

- Go into a crowded area and watch how people manage to avoid each other without giving any apparent signals. Notice what happens to cause the system to break down.

On the rare occasion that a baby's signals are persistently ignored, or misinterpreted, by their main carer, a breakdown in the relationship occurs; for example, if a baby's cry is constantly ignored they will eventually stop trying to communicate in this way and as early as 3 months will cease to cry because of the lack of response. This is a tragic example of the power of reinforcement, and how an infant's behaviour changes as a result of feedback from others and their environment. Reinforcement generally refers to the use of an event or action that strengthens or supports a particular behaviour that increases the likelihood of the behaviour being repeated, in other words something that serves as a reward. Praise can be used as reinforcement.

One of the most powerful ways to keep a behaviour going is through intermittent reinforcement, that is sometimes reinforcing behaviour and other times not. Thus, parents and carers demonstrating intermittent response to a behaviour, for example, sometimes responding to baby's cries and other times not, can result in the baby crying more frequently and being more difficult to soothe. The result of a parent or carer demonstrating intermittent response is particularly noticeable in response to an infant's or toddler's unsociable behaviour. We have all seen toddlers demanding something, such as sweets when at the shops, or for a particular toy in someone else's possession. If sometimes they get what they want in response to their demands, and sometimes they do not, their unsociable behaviour is likely to be repeated as the response to their behaviour is inconsistent. In contrast, if a toddler's unsociable behaviour is met with a consistent response of not meeting their demands, such as no sweets if demanded or having to wait their turn for a toy, the behaviour is not reinforced as the child learns there is no reward and they are less likely to continue to repeat the behaviour. The child who receives the reward sometimes but not always will continue with their demands because they are not sure if this time it will pay off, and so their unsociable behaviour is prolonged and can escalate into a full-blown tantrum. If a child's demands are always met this will also have the effect of reinforcing the unsociable behaviour and it will be repeated, but it is more likely to be short-lived and not end in a tantrum since they get their reward fairly quickly.

GROUP TASK

- Observe occasions that demonstrate intermittent responses to a young child's behaviour. The child can be any age. Note in particular the cause and consequence and why you consider it an intermittent response.

DISCUSSION POINT

Describe what you saw to others and discuss whether you agree it is an example of an intermittent response. Discuss how you consider the situation was handled and what the consequences would have been if the situation had been managed differently.

Individual variations in characteristics and development, and differences in social cultures make it difficult to identify what may be considered appropriate behaviour, but in most cultures there is usually a very fine line between what is considered socially acceptable behaviour and unsociable behaviour. Every culture has its own subculture; for example, the culture within every home is a subculture of the wider family, each having its own accepted modes of behaviour. As a child develops he or she becomes part of an increasing variety of subcultures, again each with its own principles for acceptable behaviour. The majority of these principles are generally compatible with the home environment as parents or main carers select experiences for their young children that they consider have comparable values for behaviour. But there will always be inconsistencies; for example, in the home environment a toddler may be encouraged to help tidy toys away after playing with them, but when visiting relatives this may not be expected and the toys are left on the floor and tidied away after the child has left. When the toddler is introduced into a new setting the rules may follow the rules at home or the rules at relatives' or may be different yet again, such as adults tidying the toys away while the toddler watches. There are even inconsistencies within each environment, such as paper being provided for drawing on, or notebooks for drawing in, but from the child's perspective there is no difference between this paper and any other, such as important documents. This becomes even more confusing and blatantly hypocritical in some instances when we insist on children telling the truth but then expect them to lie for the sake of a social nicety, that is, appearing grateful for a present that they neither like nor want. Both instances rely on detailed social knowledge and experience to help us deal with the ambiguity. A young child has to learn that some paper can be used for drawing and not others, but there is no universal rule to follow, and even with our considerable years of experience in knowing which paper is usually considered appropriate for drawing or writing on we still rely on our language to help us clarify such situations, asking, 'Can I write on this?' The second example demonstrates the complexity of the situation as each circumstance has its convoluted rules and has to be assessed individually. It may be socially acceptable for a young child to tell someone they do not like their cat because it scratches them, but they may not be able to say that they do not like their cat because it smells.

These social nuances create obstacles to appreciating young children's behaviour, and parents and carers can feel pressurized about what others think of their parenting or caring skills and this can be confused with that of the child's behaviour. A child's progress in becoming an individual can be hampered and, on occasion, it can become almost impossible for them to deviate from the role they have unintentionally been allocated. Many of us have experienced a parent's comments on the differences between a child's behaviour at home and the group setting. Such discrepancies become more apparent the older a child becomes, to the extent that when a child attends a pre-school group or school they can appear to be a completely different child. A common occurrence is a discrepancy between what information is provided from home regarding a child's interests and that identified when they attend group care; for example, parents may say that their child has a fascination for dinosaurs or dogs, but in the group setting the child shows only a passing interest in these things. There can be a variety of reasons for this, but that which causes the most difficulty for the child is when a role is unintentionally encouraged at home, sometimes because that is what parents want to believe, for example, their child is 'particularly advanced' or is 'always happy'.

A child may behave very differently in the setting than at home, and parents may find this difficult because it is at odds with their own view of their child. Alternatively, the child may assume the same role elsewhere and this may be a greater cause for concern because the child is continuing to live a role rather than being themselves. A child may try to demonstrate that they are 'particularly clever' and may not wish to attempt certain activities in case of failure, or they may have to suppress and deny their own feelings of sadness to show they are a 'happy' child. Under such circumstances it is apparent that if adults are experiencing difficulties in acknowledging and managing their own emotions it can be extremely problematic for young children in their care who are still learning to recognize and develop their own self-control. They can become confused, emotionally vulnerable and insecure as they battle with their own developing emotions as well as those of their main carers.

A young baby's ability to copy facial expressions is one interaction that is often undervalued and, in addition to providing the basis for communication, it has another potential benefit for the developing child: control. When we play with young babies we are apt to lead the interaction. This is a natural and appropriate response since the baby needs to learn from us, but if sometimes we copy the baby's behaviour we reverse the roles. If the baby makes a sound and we copy it, and the baby makes another sound and we repeat that, and so on, until the baby loses interest, the baby is controlling the experience and the interaction tends to be of longer duration than if we take control, and even young babies love to have control over their learning. As they mature the more control infants need to have over their learning and the more valuable the experience will be for them. A toy or piece of equipment has far greater value for the developing child if they have the opportunity to control it, to explore what it is and what it does. This is often referred to as learning through exploration or discovery, and the more control a child has the greater the learning experience.

GROUP TASK

- Sit opposite a baby of a few months old and engage their interest. When the baby utters a sound repeat as close as possible the original sound they make in pitch, tone and duration. Notice the baby's response. Continue to do this until the baby loses interest. Later repeat the activity with the same baby but with the roles reversed, that

is, try making the sounds for them to copy and notice which interaction lasts longer – when the baby leads or follows.
- Watch infants of approximately 12 months of age with a new clockwork or electronic toy that makes a sudden noise or movement. Notice their level of interest in the toy (a) when someone controls the toy so that the movement or sound is unexpected and (b) when the infant controls the sound or motion.

DISCUSSION POINT

Discuss the significance of what you observed in the above tasks and how both you and the baby can benefit from your observation.

A valuable opportunity often missed in allowing young children to take control and helping them develop their independence is when we join their play. We lack sensitivity because we do not fully value a child's play and although many practitioners will be offended by this statement and declare that they do value play, consider how often a child's play is disrupted in our desire to 'extend' or help develop progression. We do not watch and monitor how the play is developing before we 'join'. We sometimes use our power of authority to influence the play to take it where we want it to go in the name of assessment or meeting targets, and not let it go where the children were taking it. Yet, if we observed more carefully and took our cue from the children we would probably learn far more about them and their achievements. Play in its own right may well be valued as we appreciate its purpose, but fundamentally we may not be fully appreciating the child's behaviour in the play, which we may disrupt and interfere with in a way that we would never do with adults. If a group of adults were sitting around having coffee, happily chatting away, we would not plonk ourselves down without so much as an, 'Excuse me, may I join you?' We would wait to see where the conversation was going and for them to make space for us physically and socially before we added our own contributions. Anyone who lacks these social graces in adult company is not a good role model for helping children develop their social skills, but this is what frequently happens in group situations. We can still join in and extend play, usually by prolonging the interactions when they may otherwise lag, but we need to consider our position far more carefully before we attempt to participate.

Young children may have more sophisticated social skills in knowing how to join a group for the first time than we credit them with and possibly more than we 'teach' them. In such situations a child can be observed watching the group, often from the safety of a familiar adult. The more socially mature they are, the more adept they are at watching the whole play scene and waiting until they have an opportunity to contribute before making their move. They may provide a running commentary of the play they see, which may or may not be aimed at anyone in particular, but describes what they see happening. They may point to an object, or pass an object to the children in the group, sometimes retreating rapidly to the security of the familiar adult. The next stage may be to position themselves closer to the playing group, still monitoring and following the rules of the existing play and eventually joining in at an appropriate point. We often feel pressurized to coerce the child to join in and rush them before they, or the playing children, are ready, and if the timing is misjudged it disrupts the play even to the extent that the existing group disbands and the play ceases, with the adult left holding the child's hand asking other children to 'play' with him or her. By behaving in this way we take the control from the child instead of allowing the child to manage the situation in their own way, in their own time. The child may well have shown greater skill than us in handling the situation, yet we consider ourselves the experts.

Most of us live in a society that currently values knowledge, information and intelligence as something above and beyond wonder and awe, and this has led in many parts of the world to a shift from a leisurely approach of learning through discovery and play to the more hasty method of being taught through instruction. To make the instruction more agreeable it has to be made to look interesting and this is achieved by making it entertaining. Many commercially available babies' toys are now designed with limited exploratory play and can shake, rattle and roll with little, if any, effort required. Press a button and a whole sequence of manoeuvres can follow, and what does the infant do in the meantime? Sit, watch and wait. There is nothing wrong with this if we are aware that the purpose of the toy is pure entertainment, with no more value to the developing child than switching on a television. Unfortunately, in our technologically based world we are led to believe that these toys have educational value and they are often supplied as such. But the human brain is wired for problem-solving. It loves challenges and making sense of things. An example of this is how very young babies are fascinated by edges. When a bold geometric design in black and white is shown to a baby as young as 6 weeks old, they will stare intently at the shape if it is held about 20 centimetres away from their face. The attention of a 10-week-old baby can be held for a considerable length of time just looking at these geometric shapes, and the intensity of their concentration is surprising as they try to make sense of what they see. We might expect commonplace objects to be of greater interest than edges and to be of more use to help a baby make sense of the everyday world. But if we consider how disoriented we become in fog, or how a blanket of snow makes it difficult to see where one thing ends and another begins, we realize how valuable edges are in helping us make sense of things and how much we rely on them but take them for granted.

With the social and political focus on childcare in the Western world, there is so much pressure on parents and practitioners to follow approved procedures and meet targets that we can get side-tracked into focusing on young children's skills and capabilities rather than on the child themselves. We can still use observations to guide us into providing for the child's next steps and this helps us to meet statutory requirements but, more significantly, observing children provides us with the opportunity to become better acquainted with the child and to appreciate their behaviour. When we share their enjoyment in their accomplishments we can begin to value the here and now instead of always looking further ahead, so that instead of worrying so much about getting it right or wrong we can celebrate that joy, wonder and awe of caring for a new baby.

Photo 3   Dylan at 8 weeks staring intently at a bold geometric
black and white design

Further reading

Axline, V.M. (1964) *Dibs: In Search of Self.* Aylesbury; Penguin.

Faber, A. and Mazlish, E. (2001) *How to Talk so Kids Will Listen and Listen so Kids Will Talk.* London: Piccadilly Press.

National Research Council and Institute of Medicine (2000) *From Neurons to Neighborhoods: The Science of early Childhood Development.* Washington, DC: National Academy Press.

Murray, L. and Andrews, L. (2005) *The Social Baby; Understanding Babies' Communication from Birth.* Richmond: CP Publishing.

Useful websites

www.surestart.gov.uk/_doc/P0000204.pdf

www.ncb.org.uk/

SECTION 2
POLICY TO PRACTICE

SECTION 2

Policy to Practice

We are all surrounded by policies in some form or another. Irrespective of location or role, when you are working with birth to 3-year-olds there will be a policy that must be adhered to, and you can guarantee that respect for legal requirements must be demonstrated. The content of this documentation will clearly vary in accordance with the specifics of where you are and what you are doing. It could be in relation to health and safety, the learning environment, learning expectations, all three or, indeed, something quite different! Whether we like it or not we are surrounded by policy; this, however, should not impose upon our every waking hour.

This section of the book explores the reality of facilitating meaningful, stimulating and appropriate birth to 3 practice that is underpinned by current policy as necessary, drawing on the children, rather than a piece of external legislation, as the starting point. It extends from the perspective that it is the demand for highly effective practice that should drive policy, rather than policy dictating practice regardless of the needs and interests of young children and babies.

The starting point for the implementation of good quality practice should therefore be establishing a clear understanding of what we mean by 'good quality practice'. This will involve a dialogue with parents and colleagues that both examines what constitutes motivating, purposeful development and learning, and clarifies ways in which this can be achieved while respecting binding policies and procedures.

Chapter 4 focuses on holistic learning and how current policy can link to this. Anyone who has spent time with babies and young children will appreciate the fundamental need to observe children as a whole rather than a combination of parts. An 18-month-old child does not separate the colours they are learning about when painting or sharing a book at nursery from the colours they are learning about when their parents make reference to their red jumper when they are dressing them or the green cushions on the sofa. The young child is simply absorbing knowledge about colour, which will be reinforced and ultimately cemented in their long-term memory. Everything is connected, the soft touch of a blanket will evoke the same feelings of comfort gained when cuddling a favourite teddy bear. These types of sense-based reflections and connections are not exclusive to young children. The sound of a seagull can conjure up wonderful images of the sea, although we know many seagulls have now moved inland to city dwellings. Equally, smell can be incredibly evocative. Why do we find some smells wholesome, such as baking bread or newly cut grass, while others make us feel quite ill at ease? Neurological development thrives on connectivity not compartmentalization and if we are to optimize this augmentation then learning opportunities must extend from a multi-sensory, whole-child centred perspective. This chapter aims to develop a clear, in-depth, practical knowledge of child development and learning, and to investigate how babies and young children are motivated through learning. Extending from this enhanced knowledge base it is necessary to explore the day-to-day reality of the setting within which these experiences take place; which is specifically relevant in relation to how practitioners can remain true to the principle of genuine child-centred practice while respecting legislation, policies and guidelines. This is addressed in the later part of Chapter 4.

Ultimately, the greater awareness practitioners have of legislative requirements and procedures, married with a detailed understanding of the interests and needs of young children in their care, the more appropriately they will be able to facilitate the delivery of exciting and relevant experiences and environments that are underpinned, as required, by policy.

Chapter 5 considers the logistics of successfully managing legislation and policies. The nature of this management will be dependent on the setting in which you are based. The number of children in your care, the amount and type of staff, the learning environment (including inside, outside, changing areas and toilets, kitchens, storage area, to name but a few), are all contributing factors. It is important therefore to begin with a reflection of your provision in its broadest sense. Consider not only the children and how they are best catered for, but also the team of practitioners and their relative strengths, interests and personal and professional development needs. For although someone has to oversee the overall completion and compilation of all the necessary paperwork, there is no reason why elements of it cannot be delegated across the team. Legislative documentation should be seen as an embedded part of practice, which is understood and contributed to (in varying degrees as appropriate) by all who provide for the babies and young children's development and learning interests and needs. There is no reason why this cannot become a natural part of a setting's cycle of action planning and self-improvement.

A fundamental part of sustaining and enhancing this effective practice is through the establishment and implementation of practical, accessible self-evaluation tools. The essential role of continual observation and evaluation in developing babies and young children's learning experiences, and the related practicalities, are examined in Chapter 6. The chapter will open with a discussion highlighting the changing nature of early years practice, the inability to provide a fixed 'one size fits all' definition of quality and the role of self-evaluation in acknowledging these points. It will emphasize the need to establish effective process-oriented information gathering that underpins the development and learning of babies and young children. A significant part of this dialogue will involve a reflection of what is actually meant by self-evaluation and who needs to be involved in this process. The chapter goes on to reinforce the need to be inclusive at every level, sharing the documentation of children's learning journeys with the whole early years team, the parents and, most importantly, where possible, the children themselves. The content provides practical suggestions and tools to implement relevant self-evaluation. The chapter ends with a specific consideration given to the fundamental need for sensitive and supportive management of this process if it is to be effective.

4

How Current Policy Can Link to Holistic Learning

Rebecca Morton

CHAPTER OBJECTIVES

This chapter discusses:

- Interpreting policy – policy as a starting point rather than an end point.
- Keeping the spontaneity in learning.
- Developing a philosophy for the setting.

Early childhood education has become increasingly recognized as an area of great importance as a foundation for learning and for social and emotional development. The quality
of learning and care available for babies and young children has therefore been more
closely monitored and many countries have an early childhood curriculum along with
numerous other policies to try to provide children with the best possible start to their lives.
This paperwork can often seem overwhelming and makes practitioners feel as though they
are devoting more time to providing evidence for meeting government requirements than
they are to providing children with fun, enjoyable and quality learning experiences in their
early years.

Case Study

An activity is organized for a group of six children aged between 2 and 4 years. The children are to be selecting found materials for making a three-dimensional model of a farm animal. The children have all previously decided what animal they are going to be making. There are three boys and three girls. The member of staff explains to the children the purpose of the activity, then allows them to select their materials. The activity is expected to last about 10 to 15 minutes. The children actually spend an hour going through the materials. They explore the different textures; they tear up small pieces of shredded card and arrange them in a pile. They select other pieces of material and hide them in the shredded card saying they are cows and that they are hiding from the farmer. One child sings quietly to himself as he looks through the materials. Others select boxes and fill them with little pieces of material. The children all take an interest in what the others are doing and share pieces of material that they find interesting. The children speak quietly both to each other and the two members of staff in the room. When it is time to clear up only one child has selected their materials.

Case Study

An activity is organized for a group of 10 children aged between 2 years and 4 months and 3 years and 8 months. The activity has been planned and prepared in advance and involves throwing and catching games using a variety of balls and beanbags. The purpose of the session is to focus on hand–eye co-ordination. The member of staff and an additional adult helper take the children outside into a grassed area ready to start the activity. As soon as they get onto the grass, all of the children start to run around. The member of staff leading the activity allows them this opportunity to 'let off steam'. Most of the children soon stop running and break to catch their breath, however, after getting their breath back, they start running again. The adults start to set out the equipment, expecting the children to show an interest in this, but the children do not stop their running! There is a small hill in the grassed area and the children keep running to the top of the hill and then running back down it en masse, then stopping to get their breath back and repeating the run. For half an hour the children 'just' run around, by which time it is time for them to go back inside.

In both these cases the practitioners had planned a specific activity with specific learning objectives and in both cases it was decided to drop the activity and go with the moods and interests of the children. In the first instance, the practitioner made a video-recording of the children's responses because she felt that they were getting a lot more out of the experience than she had envisaged. In the second instance, the children were having so much fun simply running up and down the hill and obviously felt the need to release their energy in this way that the practitioner felt it would have been inappropriate and unproductive to stop them from doing this.

Key issues

Early years practitioners need to plan and prepare the day in advance. We need to know what we intend to do with the children in order to have the resources prepared, the other members of staff briefed, the objectives clear and to ensure that we are providing the children with a balance of learning opportunities. On the other hand, we need to provide for the individual needs of each and every child and that does not necessarily fit in with our perfectly planned days. We need to be structured and flexible. We need to have routines and spontaneity. It often seems that we need to be superhuman. Guidelines for learning in the early years tend to encourage a reflective approach to planning and implementing activities for young children and to recognize the importance of a flexible approach to teaching. Unfortunately legislative documentation also requests evidence in the form of paperwork to show long-, medium- and short-term plans for the implementation of the learning framework and how different objectives are to be met.

When it comes to education, policies and the accompanying paperwork seem to be the biggest bugbear of many a practitioner. Policies can make people fearful, change can make people fearful and making sure that we are meeting all those targets can make us fearful. As early years practitioners it is often easy to see policies as the end point, particularly those which outline learning objectives and progress targets for children. They are a series of goals that we need to guide children towards. When an infant reaches that target, we tick it off on a checklist and look to see what they need to achieve next. This is exactly what we are told not to do, but the fear of inspections by regulatory bodies makes paperwork and evidence a substantial part of our job. An example of this is England's *Practice Guidance for the Foundation Stage* (DfES, 2007), which explicitly states that the areas of Learning and Development outlined in the guidance should not be used as checklists and are not 'exhaustive'. Yet before the new framework was implemented, educational suppliers were already producing booklets breaking down each section into measurable tracking targets to assess children from birth to 5 years. How, then, can we provide young children with the fun, exciting and individualized learning experiences that they deserve while still ensuring that we meet official requirements?

When a new policy is introduced we are often greeted with the words 'it's only what you're doing already'. This is often true, but if we are stuck in the wrong mindset it is no reassurance. The learning and development of young children is often characterized by a series of benchmarks, with specific expectations for different stages of development. If we are not careful, we run the risk of becoming focused too heavily on what we deem to be 'failures'. All too often we focus on what a child cannot do, rather than what they can.

As parents we watch out for babies and children of a similar age to our own and worry that our child is not crawling yet, has not said his first words, cannot write her name, and so on. As practitioners we rejoice to have a child who soaks up information like a sponge and achieves well at everything, whereas the baby who is crawling at 7 months but spits out anything but pureed fruit is a fussy eater. He is not meeting the 'explore new foods' target. We run the risk of thinking of these children as children who cannot, rather than children who can, and as a consequence we think of ourselves as practitioners or parents who cannot too. We cannot reach that particular child in that particular area of their development, so we are failures. We need to keep in mind the fact that every child is a child who can and to learn to look for the success story in every child's life rather than highlighting their weaknesses. Both negative and positive impressions of children can influence their learning development. In other words, how that child is perceived by others becomes a self-fulfilling prophecy (Rosenthal and Jacobsen, 2003). If a child is labelled as being less competent in their speech, their language is unlikely to develop well for as long as that label remains.

GROUP TASK

Sally is 2 years 2 months old and will not eat fruit or vegetables. How can her key worker help to develop an interest in trying new foods?

Note: Does she need to taste new foods at this point?

We must not lose sight of the fact that educational policies, in particular those relating to learning and development, are there to facilitate the educational development and progress of the individual babies and children in our care. Policies are there for general guidance and should be seen as a starting point for the individualized learning process that we provide for each child. Every setting and every person within that setting, be they child, parent or practitioner, is different. A policy cannot and does not try to dictate the multitude of learning opportunities available to us. That is something that only we, as early years practitioners, can shape and decide and that in turn is influenced by the individual qualities of the children, ourselves and the settings we work in. Children learn from life, not from lists.

A policy, then, can be seen as a starting point and not an end point, something upon which we found the children's learning rather than something which we need to be working towards. This is particularly important in the development of personal, social and emotional skills. The root of all learning is in personal, social and emotional development and that goes for the adults as well as the children (Goleman, 1995). A happy, enthusiastic practitioner inspires the same qualities in the children. If you are enthusiastic about what you are doing, the children will be too. If you are bored sitting there gluing bits of tissue paper onto a flower template, why expect the children to be enjoying it any more than you?

Government policies and guidelines are introduced to ensure that pre-school settings provide a certain standard of care and education. They highlight areas of importance and they are there to improve opportunities for young children. But they are a framework rather than a philosophy. Although all practitioners working within a setting are generally aware of the government standards and general policies regarding such issues as behaviour management and child protection, it is surprising how few practitioners are knowledgeable about the individual philosophy and approach of the setting within which they work. More often than not, this is because there is no internal philosophy, because everyone is too concerned with what they feel the government thinks is important, rather than what *they* think is important.

Montessori and Steiner schools have realized the importance of emotional and spiritual development and have embraced a holistic form of learning to develop a system that has thrived for many years. A substantial element of their philosophies is the importance of care and respect for the environment and others around them. Only practitioners experienced in this approach can teach in Montessori and Steiner schools because the style of teaching is so specific. This means that all the practitioners are providing a consistent approach to the children's education both cognitively and, more importantly, emotionally and spiritually. For example, in Montessori pre-schools children are shown how to use each piece of equipment by a practitioner before they are allowed to access it freely. This is an element that is often missing from regular education systems, where the practitioners will often have their own ideas of teaching and learning. They may have chosen a nursery or school setting that most closely reflects their own philosophies, but it would be impossible to match them exactly.

If a setting can develop a distinct philosophy about the way in which they approach learning and development that is used consistently by all members of staff, they would be able to cover many of the government expectations on a regular basis. If all the staff follow the same procedures and have the same expectations, staff discussions would be more effective, as they share the same beliefs and work together as a team enabling them to interpret any new guidelines using their common understanding and values. It would thus enable them to develop a more individualized approach to more formal objectives or those that are more difficult to cover.

Different people within a setting will interact with children in different ways. Dealing with behavioural issues tends to be an area that is approached with some consistency, probably due to the fact that all settings must have a behavioural policy. But general approach to social and personal skills will differ from one person to the next and from one day to the next. For example, when a child has a runny nose, some practitioners might wipe the nose for the child, others might give them a tissue to wipe their nose themselves, another might ask them to go and get a tissue and wipe their own nose, and some may ignore the runny nose altogether.

Likewise modelling the behaviour expected of children is something that is surprisingly lacking in many establishments. An adult will ask a child to wait until they have finished a conversation with another adult or child and not to 'interrupt', but that same adult will often interrupt a conversation between two children or another adult and child with a question or direction. A unified approach to the way in which adults interact with the children in a setting can create an atmosphere of respect as children see this positive behaviour modelled.

Personal, social and emotional skills are areas of development that are relevant to every moment of every day. Current frameworks for learning in the early years identify these personal skills as a specific area for development, often emphasizing the fact that competence in personal, social and emotional abilities has a positive effect on general cognitive ability.

The development of personal care skills can easily be incorporated into the daily routine of the setting, encouraging independence, confidence, respect and self-esteem in the children. Again all staff need to be consistent in their approach and need to know who to turn to if they are unsure about how to deal with a particular situation. There is a fine balance between doing too much for children and not doing enough. On the one hand, we want to develop a child's autonomy and encourage them to take over a degree of responsibility for their own needs and interests. But, on the other hand, we do not want to give them so much responsibility that they become demotivated or frustrated.

Here are two examples of personal skills that could be incorporated into the daily routine:

- Putting a mirror on the wall, with a box of tissues next to the mirror and asking children to check their faces after eating gives them the responsibility for knowing when their face needs cleaning and when it does not, and the responsibility for doing this to a satisfactory standard. Just wiping children's faces for them or saying 'go and clean your face' without direction, takes away any of that autonomy and makes them dependent on others for something that is very easy to deal with themselves.

- When children are getting ready to go outside, those who struggle putting on their outdoor clothing may reduce the time spent outside for all of the other children, so the temptation is for adults to dress them. However, then there is no incentive for the child to learn to dress themselves. If possible they could be given the opportunity to start getting ready just a few minutes before the other children, or be given specific assistance that is gradually reduced over time.

GROUP TASK

Consider points in the daily routine of the setting where you work where children's social and personal skills could be developed. How could you ensure a consistent approach from all members of staff?

Current frameworks and approaches such as High Scope, Te Whariki, the Early Years Foundation Stage and Multiple Intelligences have accepted that there are many areas to a child's development and learning processes and that we need to provide opportunities for enabling development in all of these areas. Equal importance is attached to language, reasoning, understanding, creative, physical and personal skills alongside the health and well-being of the child. Current frameworks are designed to enable holistic learning, but actual implementation of this is not always easily recognized as people can get caught up in the fear of what they should be doing. In order to make policies more accessible for practitioners, the areas for learning and development are set out under distinct headings: in the EYFS (a framework used in England for those working with birth to 5-year-olds) these are personal, social and emotional development, communication, language and literacy, problem-solving, reasoning and numeracy, knowledge and understanding of the world, physical development and creative development. Each of these categories is then broken down into further sub-categories and then again into the ways that children might progress at different stages in their development. Although this is not a curriculum for pre-school children, it is often perceived as such. In order to make sure that they are covering all these areas in sufficient depth, practitioners often feel the need to plan specifically, with each of these areas being addressed through focused activities, rather like a school curriculum. There is nothing wrong with having regular sessions such as story times, music sessions, physical and art activities, but it is important to make sure that these organized and often highly structured sessions do not replace the freedom of an explorative approach to learning. The focus, therefore, is better to be on planning an open environment in which children can access a wide range of learning opportunities, as appropriate, rather than planning a series of 'learning activities' which require children to switch focus to the adult's goals.

Referring back to the case studies at the beginning of this chapter; in both of these organized activities the children would not have been able to enjoy and concentrate on the planned activity. In the first activity the children actually appeared to be getting more out of the learning experience than had been envisaged; the second activity, chosen by the children, was not challenging but was something that they needed to do. But in both circumstances staff felt confident to let the planned sessions drop and go with the moods of the children. Furthermore, they used the experiences to modify the way the nursery planned its day. In response to the children's behaviour in the outdoor environment, children were given more access to the open grassed area without equipment of any kind to distract them from the feeling of freedom. As a consequence of this, the practitioners noticed a definite increase in stamina over time as the children were able to run for increased periods without a break. With the indoor activity, children demonstrated a number of skills and strengths that had not previously been recognized, and their complete fascination and engagement with the materials presented to them led to the nursery setting changing the way in which they presented future similar activities. Rather than creating more work for the staff both these situations required less involvement for the staff as the children worked independently on the activities.

Photo 4.1a and b   Eleven-month-old Thomas enjoys the experience of
play with a sponge, as much as he enjoys playing with
toys that have been designed for his age and ability

In order to facilitate learning, we need to put policy into context. We need to look at what we are expected to do and make sure that we are doing that but in a way that works for us. All too often people look at the objectives for learning and then try to develop opportunities for learning that will cover these objectives. However, if there is something you are really enthusiastic about or an opportunity you would love to present to the children, it is surprising how many learning opportunities can be presented in it! This is even more easily provided for in learning experiences for younger children because their needs can be met more broadly. For example, pre-writing skills are all about fine manipulation and hand–eye co-ordination, opening up a multitude of possible activities into which this can be incorporated such as bead threading, jigsaw puzzles, sewing, sand and water play, cooking, painting, and so on. Once writing itself becomes the target, the potential for different activities becomes much more difficult.

There is a danger of learning becoming a contrived rather than a natural process. It is difficult to give examples of the spontaneous nature of learning, because observations are generally carried out with a specific purpose or focus in mind. Examples of good practice are usually well-rehearsed events, with the children and staff behaving as predicted. We need to go into planned activities with an open mind to the objectives. Just as we can get too focused on the answers we want to a specific question, we can concentrate too intently on where we want and expect an activity to go, to the detriment of other more powerful learning opportunities which may present themselves.

GROUP TASK

Think of something you enjoy doing. Develop an activity for children which you would be enthusiastic in presenting based around that interest – do not think of learning objectives while designing the activity.

After the activity has been decided see how many potential learning objectives could be achieved or developed. If necessary refine the activity to ensure that you are comfortable that the objectives would be covered in sufficient depth.

Policies are here to help us. They provide us with the basics needed for giving children a great start on their learning journeys, but no amount of written guidance can see you through a single hour of a child's life. There is nothing out there that can guide you through the perfect day, because no matter how meticulously we plan, the children will always be able to present us with a new viewpoint and a different direction in which we can take things.

DISCUSSION POINT

A baking activity has been planned for the children on the last day of term. It starts to snow outside and some of the children get extremely excited and want to go out in the snow. However, other children really want to do the baking activity. There is only time to either go outside or do the baking and there are insufficient staff to supervise one group inside and one group outside. What would you do and why?

Discuss some of the things that worry or irritate you about policies. These can be either general issues or issues that relate to a specific policy. Consider ways that these problems could be seen as advantageous.

What situations can you think of where policies make things a lot easier?

Further reading

Call, N. with Featherstone, S. (2003) *The Thinking Child (Brain-based Learning for the Foundation Stage)*. Stafford: Network Educational Press.

Goleman, D. (1995) *Emotional Intelligence: Why It can Matter More than IQ*. London: Bloomsbury.

Useful websites

www.minedu.govt.nz – for information on Te Whariki New Zealand Early childhood education curriculum

5

Managing Legislation and Policy

Mike Carter

CHAPTER OBJECTIVES

- Understand the context of the EYFS policy.
- Understand key priorities for England.
- Use legislation and provision to maximize children's development, for example by collecting information about the outcomes for children.

This chapter looks at the changes in legislation and the introduction of the Early Years Foundation Stage requirements and guidance for provision for children from birth to 5. This strategy combines notions of welfare for children with those of intellectual development. The chapter seeks to suggest some of the reasoning that underpins the EYFS and looks at how different settings and provision may adapt and profit from it for children up to 3 years old. The chapter also develops ideas about promoting high quality provision, particularly through continuing professional development for staff and through self-evaluation and external inspection. The importance of observation and assessment are stressed since the impact of provision can only be known by observing its outcomes in terms of the children's development. The chapter ends with three discussion points that are central to any setting's adoption of the EYFS and to the further improvement of very young children's development.

Case Study

A London nursery centre has mixed provision and takes babies and children under 3 as well as 3-year-olds. It opens for 10 sessions a week, and it serves an area with low socio-economic backgrounds and a small but growing minority ethnic population. Over a number of years it has grown in effectiveness and the range of its provision. In 1999, an OFSTED inspection report stated that the centre provided a quality and standard of educational provision that were 'acceptable'. The centre was given one main issue to improve, which was to 'enhance assessment, by ensuring all entries indicate the progress the children make and that records are being regularly maintained'. By 2004 the centre provided 'good' childcare and had improved its assessment systems and records. Growth had enabled the employment of better qualified staff. The centre had been hoping for more advice coming from its inspection. What was written in the report of the 2004 inspection provided little to improve, but the inspector fed back a minor issue that the centre might consider the balance of child-initiated and child-provided activities for its oldest children. The staff discussed this at length and made adjustments to the sessions accordingly. The inspection of 2008, combined the inspection of day care standards and of nursery education. It found that provision under each of the Every Child Matters outcomes was good and that the centre had made further improvements since the previous inspection. The inspector found that the quality and standards of nursery education were 'outstanding'.

In this example, over a number of years the nursery centre had made steady improvements. It was working in a low socio-economic area with a growing number of children from homes where English is an additional language. The improvements stemmed in part from the inspection outcomes. Inspection was treated as a way to improve rather than a stick with which to be hit. The impact of inspection improved as day care was inspected alongside nursery education. However, the centre did not just wait for inspections, it started to evaluate itself and, in 2005, began using a form and collecting information that would provide evidence for its own conclusions about effectiveness. The staff themselves have found that discussions about evidence and drawing conclusions have been most interesting and provide a strong rationale for what they do and how they talk with others. Such a sense of direction is very empowering. Parents, too, are largely delighted with their children's development and the way in which the centre cares for their need to share information about their children.

The context of policy

Quality counts

There is much research suggesting that the quality of provision for the under-5s makes a very significant difference to its impact. It suggests that poor-quality provision may be even worse than no provision at all. This challenging finding gives legitimacy and credence to those who have invested in high-quality provision or training in its provision. The UK government frequently includes the word 'quality' when discussing provision for very young children, and this has a specific meaning concerning provision that maximizes children's development.

British outcomes

The urgency of improving the range, the rigour and the reach of high-quality provision for very young children cannot be overemphasized. Often, the increase of childcare opportunities has been justified by a political imperative to increase the number of parents in work. Part of the reasoning behind this is that there is a very strong statistical link between low academic attainment and poverty, resulting in further unemployment and a cycle of deprivation. Cultural changes may have decreased the confidence of parents in child-rearing. Many are unclear what is reasonable and are sceptical about the balance of acquiescence and parental control in the current context. The aspirations of some families concern material goods and short-term satisfaction. In countries such as Finland, with better educational outcomes, communities seem to have a strong culture of nurturing the young. In the UK, young children often have to fit their lives around adult preferences. Such features, added to societal pressures from the press, the instabilities of relationships, a testing regime in schools and the inadequacies of political support to eliminate child poverty, have developed a culture that undermines the real needs of childhood. Consequently, some of our youngest children are raised in inappropriate circumstances. The need is to provide the nurture that young children require and to help parents to support their children's development effectively. Several measures introduced by Parliament endeavour to help this cause.

The framework of provision

There are a good variety of ways in which babies and young children are cared for that have often been considered as *care* in terms of enabling children's physical needs and happiness. This is often provided in the child's own home by a nanny or a relative. However, increasingly it is provided in a childminder's home (often with a very small number of other children, or the childminder's own children). The quality of this care has been variable, with the best helping the children to live happily and grow physically and intellectually, sometimes providing better support than their parents. Despite having a baby, more parents are deciding to continue to work and the proportion of single parents needing to work has grown as well. Consequently, government measures to increase the availability of childcare places has resulted in greater diversity, with more nurseries and other settings providing for babies and very young children. However, there is very uneven availability in many areas. As part of the extended schools' programme, designed to support the Every Child Matters outcomes, schools are being required to provide day care for children and pupils, or to provide

Table 5.1   Overall quality judgement categories, by type of setting

Type of setting or provision	Percentage achieving the judgement					Number inspected
	Outstanding (%)	Good (%)	Satisfactory (%)	Inadequate: notice of action to improve (%)	Inadequate: enforcement action (%)	
Childminder	3.6	57.6	37.5	2.2	0	43,741
Full day care	3.4	62.5	32.0	2.0	0.1	8,938
Sessional day care	2.2	62.2	33.3	2.3	0.1	6,043
Out of school day care	0.9	48.0	46.9	4.1	0.1	6,174
Crèche day care	2.2	47.8	47.8	2.2	0.0	900
Multiple day care	2.5	60.8	34.9	1.6	0.2	2,811

Note: Caution is needed in the interpretation of such statistics, especially where the numbers of inspections are relatively small.

Source: OFSTED (2008).

a directory of such local services. This provision is designed to be provided year round, from 8 a.m. until 6 p.m. In its reviews of such services, OFSTED defines six types of provision:

- Childminder – registered to look after one or more children at home, for up to two hours a day.
- Full day care – not in homes but provides for four hours care or more (includes day nurseries).
- Sessional day care – not in homes, and for less than four hours.
- Out of school care – provides day care before school, after school or during holidays.
- Crèches – providing occasional care needing registration for over five days a year.
- Multiple cay care – providing more than one type of care, for example, full day + sessional.

These categories were devised for the purpose of inspections after April 2005. The Office for Standards in Education's inspection data shows wide variations in the quality of provision by region and type of setting (Table 5.1).

Table 5.1 uses data from inspectors' judgements made between 1 April 2005 and 31 December 2007 in England and shows that there can be either excellence or inadequacy within each type of childcare. The high proportion of 'satisfactory' judgements in each type suggests a worryingly high degree of mediocrity while, for the children involved, any setting with an inadequate 'judgement' is unacceptable. The focus of the EYFS is likely to be more broadly based upon provision for the whole child and not just the previous care requirements. The impact this may have on the figures in Table 5.1 will be interesting and, hopefully, will suggest improvements to the nurture we offer our young children.

Policy initiatives

The hope that good early child-rearing and nurture could reduce antisocial behaviour and later social expenditure seemed to offer support and hope for all. The difficulty is in implementing good early child-rearing practices within periods of cultural change. In response to this and the apparent need for a better educated adult population, the government has been introducing policies at high speed that subsume earlier ones. Some of these policies seek to draw together previously unrelated guidance, while others are implemented through new legislation. There are additional policies that are couched in terms of guidance only.

Perhaps the most significant overarching policy is that of the ECM outcomes framework. It promotes five simple aspirations that we would all wish to see for children, that is, that they are healthy, safe, achieving, contributing and have some economic security. The implications of these are then detailed in terms of the different ways they may be achieved. They are for all children of any age. Other policies and requirements can be subsumed by one or more of the outcomes. They cover all areas previously thought of as 'care' and all those concerning 'education'. The Children's Plan (DCSF, 2007) is another recent initiative that draws together many previous programmes and policies, and gives them new priority, largely fitting within the broad headings of the ECM outcomes as well. Some policies have been strengthened by new laws, such as concerns for the safeguarding of children. The inspection of care as well as education has involved OFSTED in carrying out single inspections, thereby avoiding the previous duplication by local authority services.

Through this picture of policy formation, a number of particular trends of policy can be discerned. There is a desire to *increase the number of care places* and this is leading to more diversification and competition in the private sector. It also suggests the need for more information and guidance for parents. Research suggests a need to *improve the quality of parenting* perhaps through more Sure Start facilities and more emphasis on the part schools play. What impact do settings have on how parents nurture their children? Where provision is weaker the *quality of care needs to be improved*; for example, more rigour in appointing staff and providing professional development. This suggests accurate evaluations of the children's and the setting's needs. There is also a need to *increase consistency in the quality* and availability of provision. Self-evaluation and the inspection framework can ensure the required standards are met as well as prompting high quality. *Increased opportunities are needed* in more deprived areas to militate against cycles of disadvantage. Targeted projects such as Sure Start are supporting this, particularly as settings can maximize the use of any locally available initiatives or funding. Politicians seek to *provide more parental choice*, for example by providing care to enable both parents to have a choice about work. Some professionals believe that this could lead to parents abrogating their responsibilities for their children. A number of high-profile cases point to the need to *strengthen the safeguarding of children*. Every Child Matters policies are not yet working well enough to overcome these dangers and all authorities, settings and schools need regular evaluation of systems and of training. *There is a call for greater accountability*, especially as the public purse is increasingly used and as parents look for more information. Objective monitoring and self-evaluation complement the external inspection system. *A greater use of assessment of children's development is advocated*. This is not the ticklist system decried by many but observations to check how each child is developing and their next needs. A strategy that schools are finding particularly helpful is that of *better partnerships* with other schools, and the rewards are increasingly important. Many children attend several different settings in a week and more agencies and services need to share information. The potential for professional development and moderation is high.

Early Years Foundation Stage and Every Child Matters outcomes

The two major delineating policy initiatives that have direct implications for young children and babies are the Every Child Matters and the Early Years Foundation Stage frameworks (Figure 5.1).

The ECMs outcomes are five all-encompassing aspirations for children and young people. They seek to raise the awareness of everyone involved with children and young people both throughout and across their lives. While their initial motivation concerned child protection, they aspire to address any barrier to learning and free development that children may suffer. In practice they rely on adults extending their concern and proactively providing for children's needs. This may mean that various services need to work together to ensure provision.

This powerful and idealistic set of aspirations has not achieved instant success. The children's outcomes rely to some extent on services working more closely together. This was foreseen by the government and a range of measures is promoted to enable inter-service collaboration, including the sharing of information. However, change has been slow and in some cases local authority services are still unable to collaborate quickly. Despite such criticism of their implementation, the five ECM outcomes provide a strong basis for reductions in barriers to children's development and learning.

Every Child Matters outcomes framework

- **Be healthy:** physically, mentally and emotionally, healthy lifestyles, sexually healthy, choose not to take illegal drugs. Eating and learning to eat well, being happy, learning profitably, being sensibly cautious of danger, and so on.
- **Stay safe:** from maltreatment, neglect, violence, and sexual exploitation, from accidental injury and death, bullying and discrimination, crime and antisocial behaviour and have security, stability and are cared for, avoiding dangers, lack of abuse, harm, or exposure to danger.
- **Enjoy and achieve:** ready to learn, attend and enjoy the setting, achieve appropriate capabilities for age, personal and social development and enjoy recreation and increasing capabilities.
- **Make a positive contribution:** begin to make choices, enjoy routines and positive behaviour, develop positive relationships and begin to understand others, develop self-confidence and successfully deal with significant challenges.
- **Achieve economic well-being:** live in decent homes and sustainable communities, have access to transport and material goods, live in households free from low income, start to communicate with others and begin the process of gaining basic skills.

Experience suggests that the best settings make rich and varied provision for each of the five areas and the staff review the children's outcomes. This helps them see which provision is most effective, how it can improve, how the setting can support parents in complementing the child's experiences and how they can use the information gained for self-evaluation. Reviewing the children's actual outcomes may be difficult and certainly should prompt a

Every Child Matters

(The overarching set of five aspirations we have for all children and young people)

Be Healthy   Stay Safe   Enjoy and   Make a   Economic
                            Achieve   Positive   Well-being
                                         Contribution

A few examples of initiatives are:

Healthy   Staff checks;   Personalized   School   Widening
schools;   CRBs   learning;   council;   participation;
sport   new curricula   eco schools   extended
                                                              schools

Many of the strategies to accomplish the above form aspects of:

The Children's Plan

(A bringing together and re-positioning of previous policies, guidance and strategies for children.)

One such major policy initiative is the:

Early Years Foundation Stage (EYFS)

(For under-5s – integrating 0–3 and 3–5 guidance and care requirements)

Other legislation and regulations include, for example:

Childcare Bill   **Sure Start**   **CYPP**
(Strengthening   (Financed provision for   (Local authority
requirements +   under-5s and families in   strategies)
partnerships)   targeted areas)
                                                      LSCB
                                                      (Local Safeguarding
                                                      Children's Boards)

OFSTED inspections
(These now cover most settings and provision, including Joint Area Reviews of the work of local authorities. Inspectors use the five ECM outcomes to judge provision.)

Figure 5.1   How some major policies relate to each other

Form: A: Suggested form for recording ECM <u>outcomes</u> for individual children.

Setting............Group.............Staff member............Dates completed:

Does the child appear to be achieving these outcomes? put ✗, ✓ or ? Add comment/evidence where appropriate.

Name:	Safe from harm	Healthy	Enjoy and achieve	Positive contribution	Economic well-being

Figure 5.2   Form A: Recording ECM outcomes

professional discussion. A simple way is to consider each child and each of the outcomes, and simply recording basic information, such as in the form in Figure 5.2.

This form has the advantage of simplicity and is helpful in settings with a larger number of children. It prompts staff to consider the child's situation rather than the setting's provision for each of the five outcomes. It can provide simple yet effective feedback about key issues for pupils and may lead to significant concerns about safeguarding or other ECM outcomes as described by the Common Assessment Framework (CAF). The form in Figure 5.3 links provision to outcomes and may support self evaluation by the setting.

Together these forms provide a setting with helpful evidence to evaluate its provision. They prompt practitioners to observe and consider what is working well. They encourage a more evidence-based approach to care and development. However, more detailed information would be required to track the development and progress made by individual children, and here the Early Years Profile gives helpful suggestions. For some settings these forms may provide helpful evidence for self-evaluation.

The Early Years Foundation Stage

This comprises a specific set of recommendations for the nature and content of the development of children under 5. For the first time it provides support for a seamless growth, taking in both the previous Birth to Three and the Three to Five Guidance. In addition, it incorporates the previous 'standards of care'. This helpfully prioritizes what we know about learning; for example, it is very fast in the early years and it takes place along with everyday living. We also know that provision for welfare cannot be separated from provision for learning.

A central idea is that of assessment. While statutory requirements concern the completion of 'pupil profiles' by the end of the Foundation Stage (that is, the Reception Year), many think that some form of assessment is necessary much earlier. Such an idea has alarmed others who think that this suggests tests and tick lists even for babies. However, in a sense many parents themselves do this intuitively by noticing their child's development both physically and intellectually – some to the extent of comparison with norms or anxiety with different progress levels. Much research suggests that an integral part of making good provision for any child, or group of children, is observing their behaviour and their reaction to what is provided: 'observe children sensitively and respond appropriately to encourage and extend curiosity and learning, to tune into rather than talk at, children, taking a lead and direction from what the children say or do … All planning starts with observing children' (DfES, 2007: 16). This is the best way to consider their development and how next to provide for their needs (using the word 'provide' in the broadest sense to include the environment, objects, atmosphere and adult actions as well as talk).

The EYFS promotes assessments as simple, everyday observations that contribute to tomorrow's plan. However, such notes can also be used to contribute to a periodic review of a child's development and help towards the summative end of Foundation Stage assessment. Guidance in considering developments and broad expected stages is provided within the *Foundation*

Form B.

Every Child Matters – Provision and Outcomes <u>Individual Staff</u>

		Provision made	Outcomes evidence
Be safe from	Maltreatment and neglect Violence and exploitation Injury Bullying and discrimination Crime and Antisocial behaviour Insecurity and instability Lack of care		
Be healthy	Physically Mentally Emotionally Healthy lifestyle Sexually Drugs-free		
Enjoy and achieve	Ready for school Attend and enjoy Achieve academically and otherwise Personal and social Recreation		
Positive contribution	Decision-making Environment Positive behaviour Relationships Empathy Confidence Resilience Enterprising		
Economic well-being	Decent home Sustainable community Access to transport Access to facilities Ready for further education Preparing for employment Free from poverty		

Figure 5.3   Form B: Provision and outcomes

Stage Profile Handbook (QCA, 2003). Like all such guidance, professionals need to use written comparators with their knowledge and good experience of children's development. It is hoped that practice and guidance will improve with more experience.

The EYFS uses four 'themes' by which to group its 16 principles:

1   The theme called '**The unique child**' reminds us that:

   - Each child is an individual and develops holistically. Children do not grow by adult-imposed categories.
   - Another principle is that of inclusivity: that each child is accepted and treated with equal respect.
   - The desire to keep children safe, introduces the notion that their resilience grows when their well-being is protected.
   - A fourth principle concerns children's health and well-being.

2   The four principles outlined under the theme '**Positive relationships**' are:

   - 'Respecting each other' especially the feelings of children and their families.
   - 'Parents as partners' implies that they know their children best and collaboration is very productive.
   - 'Supporting learning' suggests that warm trusting relationships help development.
   - 'A key person' with which each child can build a strong link.

3   Under the theme '**Enabling environments**' the first principle is:

   - 'Observation, assessment and planning' through which children's individuality may be best served.
   - 'Supporting every child' suggests how the child's environment 'in and out of the setting' (DfES, 2007: 9) will influence development one way or another. What adults do now with children will affect the twenty-second century.
   - 'The learning environment' suggests how children need challenges and support appropriate to them.
   - 'The wider context' suggests the value to be gained by collaborating with other settings or the community.

4   The last four principles are grouped under the theme '**Learning and development**':

   - 'Play and exploration' reflects the convincing research into the importance and variety of play.
   - 'Active learning' reminds us of the value of involvement, doing things and doing them with others.
   - 'Creativity and critical thinking' helps us help children to make new connections and to enquire.
   - 'Areas of learning and development' comprise six domains of learning and bear only some resemblance to school subjects. They provide a tried and tested way of categorizing.

Combining welfare and education standards

The new learning and development requirements outlined in the EYFS include:

1   The Early Learning Goals (ELGs) working towards the end of the Foundation Stage aspirations for attainment.
2   The educational programmes categorized under the six interconnected areas of learning.
3   Assessment arrangements for under 3-year-olds:

   - comprise making systematic observations
   - comprise using these to identify and plan experiences
   - have in mind the ELGs to which development can proceed
   - must make any relevant records available as they relate to the EYFS Profile. They should enable moderation to aid the accuracy of observations and assessments.

The welfare requirements

These are much more numerous and specific. There are three categories:

1   Overarching **general legal requirements**, for example, data collection regulations or employment law;
2   **Specific legal requirements**, such as keeping written risk assessments or assigning a key person to each child.
3   **Statutory guidance**, such as providing for a two-way flow of information with parents or ensuring staff are aware of the need for confidentiality at times.

Owing to continued breaches of trust and harm to some children by care professions, there is a range of legal requirements about staff:

   - All staff must have enhanced CRB (in full) checks.
   - Settings must keep records of such checks.
   - They must have other systems to ensure practitioners are suitable to work with children.
   - They must have regard to requirements of the Safeguarding Vulnerable Groups Act 2006.
   - They must inform OFSTED of changes, such as personnel, times, premises, and so on.
   - Staff must meet qualification requirements.

These training and experience requirements make a compromise between the largely untrained workforce and a high number of those who are trained. The recognition that child carers are also implicit educators suggests a much higher level of training and awareness is needed. The Children's Workforce Development Council (CWDC) is promoting higher levels but settings, practitioners and individuals should be more responsible for their own continuing professional development (CPD). New roles such as 'key persons', 'lead professional' (a term coined by the Every Child Matters agenda for a person designated to oversee the provision made to help a child with specific barriers to achieve the outcomes), and parental support are providing new challenges for which their training is needed. It is hard to overstate the importance of further training. Smaller settings often find greater difficulty in providing professional development. Typically, the larger the setting, the more flexible in terms of finance and logistics.

Continuing professional development can take place in a variety of ways. Informally, practitioners can observe other adults and learn from each other although this is heightened when discussed and with a focus. Professional books and journals and DVDs also offer an increasing base for staff learning. However, practitioners are attending formal courses more frequently. Some of these are spread over longer periods. Visits to another setting are very rewarding, especially where provision is for small numbers. External consultants can also provide specific needs and inspiration for improvement. Formal, externally accredited courses/assessments provide strong learning (for example, Early Years Professional) and the range of degree and diploma courses is constantly increasing. Some of these courses are very specific while others provide good general learning concerning working with children. Most are significant commitments but provide the best rewards.

The professional development of childminders and those from very small settings is likely to be difficult, first, in gaining the information to meet all the requirements, as suggested earlier in this chapter, and second, in finding the money and the time to enable their CPD. Yet the smaller settings have excellent potential for high impact on children's development. The status and financing of childminders should be improved urgently. Sue Learner (2008: 13) identifies the difficulty: 'Nancy Stewart, early years consultant at Shropshire County Council, has got round the problem by holding the training for childminders on a Saturday. She would like to see childminders being given paid days for training, just as teachers are with inset days.' The EYFS makes explicit recognition of small and home-based settings such as childminders.

The inspection regime

The inspection of provision for all pupils under 5 is now carried out by one inspectorate: OFSTED. This reflects the combining of care and educational provision under the EYFS and requirements will no longer be checked by local authorities. Inspections under the EYFS start in September 2008 and all registered settings, including childminders, are subject to inspection.

The Office for Standards in Education has extensive inspection experience and subcontracts most of its inspections to regional inspection service providers (RISPs). Albeit largely from school inspections, this extensive experience has led to a number of conclusions from which settings may draw.

1   **Honest self-evaluation helps realistic inspection outcomes.** Inspectors value sound well-based self-evaluations, for example, of pupils' development physically and in terms of skills and learning.

2   **Benchmarking aids objectiveness.** Knowing how children's development compares with others of the same age helps identify priorities and informs discussion with parents. In addition, knowledge of the provision made by other settings aids competitiveness.

3   **Good quality care helps to support children's development and their learning.** The Office for Standards in Education often found that learning improves with greater levels of child welfare.

4   **Where they are possible, 'measurements' help to evaluate developments.** The many quantifiable measures of children's development, for example, height, eating, talk frequency, and so on, provide strong indications of growth and progress.

5   **Observing the outcomes helps settings (and OFSTED) to evaluate the provision and plan for the future.** Looking at how children respond provides better indications of success than just recording what is provided.

6   **Self-evaluation is best when it is used to *improve* provision – not just to 'prove' provision.** Self-evaluation is best when it is integrated into everyday practice and is simple and manageable (see Chapter 6).

The Office for Standards in Education already has a unique position to enable reviews on a national scale of the quality and impact of early years provision. Previous reviews have been critical of some aspects such as the 7 per cent of extended school services and the 8 per cent of crèches which were inadequate. In addition, some 125,000 children are left with childminders or nurseries that were no better than satisfactory (Ward, 2007). More should be expected of the services provided to support children's development. Inspectors are greatly helped by a well-evidenced self-evaluation. For some time, schools have been expected to provide a completed self-evaluation form (SEF) online and, at the time of writing, OFSTED is piloting such a form for early years settings. This form is unlikely to be a requirement but appears as an expectation. Currently, self-evaluation is an option that larger settings choose as it provides a good sense of purpose and development for the setting. (See the case study earlier in this chapter.)

Pertinent questions that may support children's development

Provision or outcomes

In the early days of inspection, schools experienced difficulties because they knew how hard they worked and what they provided, yet the inspection judgements seemed to ignore this. What inspections actually looked at was the outcomes, that is, how much the children had learned and how developed their SMSC skills had become. (Spiritual, moral, social and cultural development is still inspected by law in schools.)

GROUP TASK

How can you identify and gauge outcomes from the provision that you make?
(Hint: List the records that you already keep and see what they suggest.)

Consider the forms of feedback you already get from children, parents, others. Can these be increased/formalized to add rigour? Consider the progress made and contrast this with norms for each child. Make sure you have considered finding evidence for each of the five ECM outcomes

Now list and match up all the things you do to help the children.

'Hearing' the partners

In other chapters the importance of observing and listening to children is outlined. Other stakeholders, such as parents and staff, often have views that settings need to address. Settings and providers need to collect these views. Often such opinions will inform the self-evaluation and help to prioritize improvements. The increasing number of children using more than one care setting/carer also suggest the importance of collaboration with other settings. We must ask 'What is a full day in this child's life, like?'

The importance of assessment and monitoring

In this chapter the need for self-evaluation is stressed. Being aware of the impact of what is provided and how it compares with other settings is empowering information. It provides clear improvement priorities as well as identifying needs for individual or groups of children. Only with simple but manageable systems to assess children's outcomes and monitor the setting's effectiveness can self-evaluation for inspection and self-use be accomplished.

GROUP TASK: INCLUSION, BARRIER IDENTIFICATION AND ECM OUTCOMES

One by one consider a day in the life of each child. (You could do this task over several days.)

What acted as barriers or aids to their learning and development? Are there implications for their ECM outcomes? Are there things you can do to make each child's chances more equal?

The EYFS Profile and statutory requirements (for managers)

The EYSF Profile and guidance provide helpful criteria and a degree of benchmarking. Whatever the size of the setting the essential task of caring for and helping children develop must be managed and monitored. All staff need this sense of mission and should reject barriers to growth such as comments asking, 'What can you expect with those parents?' The process of inspection also needs calm and careful management. As the case study suggests, inspection can and should be a developmental experience. Honesty, collaboration and the use of findings enable the inspection to be helpful.

Self-evaluation

In order that inspection works well, the robustness of a setting's own self-evaluation can provide strong support. Currently, the completion of a self-evaluation form is an option. Nevertheless, the persistent value of self-evaluation lies in how it raises awareness of relative strengths and aspects for improvement. It relies on monitoring outcomes through assessments as well as checking provision and ensuring statutory requirements are met and children's ECM outcomes maximized. The OFSTED form is likely to be available online for completion and the information in it used to plan the next regular inspection. New forms can be submitted at any time to update the information contained.

Using inspection

Clear-sighted leaders or managers often see inspection as a free consultancy. Establishing an early mutuality with the inspector(s) is important. Most inspectors draw on their extensive relevant experience but their priority is to make judgements based on the inspection criteria (which are publicly available at www.ofsted.gov.uk). Inspectors' views deserve respect, consistent as they usually are with broad-based experience. Very occasionally judgements may need explanation, which good inspectors are happy to give. However, on rare occasions they do not 'add up', and here settings should not fear making formal complaints. Inspection records that have little difference from the setting's self-evaluation indicate valid monitoring. Where there are significant differences, settings should consider the efficacy of their monitoring and evaluation strategies. In any event the key issues, and any discernible, minor ones, should provide real impetus and urgency for improvements.

Providing continuing professional development

In one sense the needs of children do not change over time. However, their situations and the influences on them and their parents do change. For example, there have been changes to the proportions of children from various backgrounds. Also what children see, experience and can do changes with the current trends and attitudes. Consequently, all staff need to recognize new needs and find the most effective ways to meet them. Continuing with strategies from previous periods will often not work. Also, much more is now known about effective ways to promote children's physical and mental development. Settings or adults that make little effort to employ the most effective ways of promoting children's development are letting their children down.

It is well known that the quality of care and provision for children has been too variable. This can seriously undermine the equality of children's start in life. The best settings provide a high degree of learning for their staff. In an earlier section, some ways that staff can gain new knowledge and understanding were outlined. Many practitioners are likely to need to learn about the EYFS principles and practice as well as the ECM outcomes. New practices in safeguarding, assessment, self-evaluation and working with parents are also areas to develop and may require external CPD.

DISCUSSION POINT

1   How can the setting approach the need for a balance of time spent indoors and out of doors – bearing in mind safety and risk assessments as well as the children's need to explore?

2   Given the setting's (or provision's) size and limitations, how can CPD be provided for staff? The essential learning that adults make is one of the few 'levers for improvement'. How can time, finance and inclination be maximized to promote learning?

3   Given the importance of self-evaluation (SE), how can assessment, evidence, monitoring and analysis be built into everyday practice that can then inform future improvements in the settings' provision and the children's development? First review the SE requirements of OFSTED and then consider what information will be needed to supply the SEF with sufficient rigour, including both what is provided and the outcomes in terms of children's actual development.

Further reading

Abbot, L. and Langston, A. (2005) *Birth to Three Matters: Supporting the Framework of Effective Practice*. Maidenhead: Open University Press.
Bruce, T. and Meggitt, C. (2002) *Child Care & Education*. Oxford: Hodder and Stoughton.
Cheminais, R. (2006) *Every Child Matters: A Practical Guide for Teachers*. London: David Fulton.
Waterman, C. and Fowler, J. (2004) *Plain Guide to the Children Act 2004*. Slough: NFER.

Useful websites

www.ofsted.gov.uk

www.everychildmatters.gov.uk

www.standards.dcsf.gov.uk

6

Establishing Efficient Self-Evaluation Tools

Jan Foreman

CHAPTER OBJECTIVES

The aim of this chapter is to share some practical suggestions to self-evaluate the impact of the service you provide for the effective development and learning of children. By the end of this chapter you will have a clear understanding of:

- What self-evaluation is.
- Why an effective process is of benefit to the whole team.
- Practical suggestions and tools to implement a process.

Part of the success of any organization is the need for the whole team to be involved in reviewing its performance and evaluating their current position. The reasons for this include:

- reflecting on the effectiveness of the adults' teaching, practice and experiences offered to the children
- analysing and reviewing the direct impact this has on children's development and learning
- motivating and empowering the team to believe in themselves and be less fearful of change
- improving the quality of the provision.

We need to consider that team members are more likely to perform well and have better motivation to progress if they are supported by a strong team of managers and colleagues who are devoted to developing the skills of observation, reflection and analysis.

Change is inevitable and, when it happens, the team members involved will need to consider how easily they are able to adapt; whether it be to new children attending, staff changes, local or government initiatives or alterations in inspection processes. Having a clear process for self-evaluation can not only assist in monitoring the impact of change, but also will accustom team members to change itself. Introducing a self-evaluation process can increase confidence in team members to question their practice. This is as a result of using their developing skills of observation to reflect and evaluate. This information can result in them using the prompts to change opportunities and routines that they felt were not working or not of good quality.

Establish the definition of good quality

Within the early years there has been much debate on the definition of good quality. Abbott and Langston (2004) cite Moss and Pence who argue that 'quality in childcare is a constructed concept, subjective in nature and based on values, beliefs and interest rather than an objective and universal reality. Quality childcare is, to a large extent, in the eye of the beholder' (1994: 5).

The team can begin to develop its own definitions of quality by sharing these during team meetings and the development of a mission statement. We also need to consider that the team within is more likely to perform well and have motivation to progress if it is supported by a strong team of managers and colleagues who are devoted to developing the skills of observation, reflection and analysis.

GROUP TASK

As a team discuss your current process of documenting children's development and learning. Consider and debate:

- How effective do all members of the team believe your current system is being?
- How much of the current system is actually used to record children's development?
- Do team members believe that the current system is a productive use of their time?
- How is this information shared with the relevant people, carers and parents?

The children's learning is effective

Experts in the field of early years have long been secure in the knowledge that children's learning is enhanced and consolidated through play. Claxton and Carr (2004: 88), with reference to Dweck (1999), go as far as to suggest that 'what is clear is that early childhood centres and schools do change children's learning orientations, for better or worse (Dweck 1999) and it is risky to pretend otherwise. There is always a learning curriculum, and it can steer students towards or away from developing the attributes of effective learning'. If we are to agree with Claxton and Carr, then the play environment for young children will have a huge impact on their learning and interests. As skilled practitioners it is our role to offer children as many opportunities as our setting permits to push out the boundaries of opportunities and to discover the breadth of learning as much as we can. Moyles (1989: ix) suggests that 'Play at its best in educational situations, provides not only a real medium for learning but enables discerning and knowledgeable adults to learn more about children and their needs'.

Adults can adopt the use of observation to question how the children are accessing and exploring these opportunities and resources, and can identify what learning is taking place and in turn offer an opportunity for children to extend this learning by developing further opportunities or resources, hence facilitating the play. Regular use of observations carried out at various times of the day in different situations will provide us with a wealth of information about individual babies and children. As this observation-based knowledge regarding the way individual children learn is gained we can facilitate this learning by offering the appropriate stimuli.

Case Study

The staff in a toddler room of a private day nursery observed that the children predominantly played in the role-play corner; this was a small area in the corner of the play room. The children were aged between 1 year and 3 months and 2 years and 6 months. The staff's observations reinforced their knowledge that many young children within this developmental stage would reluctantly share their resources. The staff subsequently made the decision to dedicate the whole of this playroom to role play to include the home corner equipment, dolls, blankets, cots, feeding equipment, nappies, cleaning cloths, dressing up in everyday clothing, shoes, hats, scarves and handbags. There was also a small comfortable den, made from a large, inexpensive piece of fabric, in the corner of the room.

The case study demonstrates that by using observations to reflect on children's interests, and the adults sharing their findings, they were able to plan effectively for the group. The staff provided plentiful resources, many of these duplicated. Adapting the environment to suit the children's interests reduced conflict and provided a less cramped play space where the play was more focused and persistent.

Montessori suggested that a young child's nursery environment should be one of silence. By this she was not advocating that children should be seen and not heard but that babies and children, who are concentrating and focused on their play, are frequently quiet because they are so absorbed in their activity; thus if all children are quiet the environment fosters their learning and is stimulating. The key point to take away from this is that Montessori demonstrated that the learning environment should evolve in genuine response to the children's interests and needs. Bruce (2004:135) makes reference to the importance of child initiated, free flow play but also suggests that many group settings offer sessions 'in which children are guided in their play into pre-structured adult-led outcomes'. While there is a need to guide play, over-structured, planned activities with specific aims, objectives and learning intentions for children to achieve, do not always enhance a child's learning. In the writer's experience practitioners have suggested that if the activity does not deliver the intended learning outcome it is deemed not to be successful; thus setting targets of success or failure. Practitioners spend many hours planning these structured activities, frequently during their own, unpaid, time. If these experiences are founded purely on external guidelines without any informed, evaluative underpinning reflecting the children's actual developmental stage, they risk making a futile contribution to the actual learning. It could therefore be argued that practitioners' time could be better spent.

Most providers working with babies and young children will have given much consideration to the layout of play space, flexible routines and shared the most appropriate times to suit individual preferences with parents. The daily routines, carried out by a sensitive, caring adult, will provide wonderful learning opportunities whether you are eating a meal, changing a nappy, singing or sharing books together. It is therefore important that the team spends time reflecting on the value of these learning opportunities and does not discount them.

GROUP TASK

Consider the current daily routines of the babies and children in your care.
Having compiled a list of these routines, discuss what potential for learning there is during these times.

GROUP TASK

Consider how you may effectively observe children over the period of a session/day. These observations will vary according to several factors:

- consider what information you actually need to gain from these observations
- the number of children being cared for in a room – the lower the number of children the more likely it is that anecdotal observations would be more beneficial than formal written records
- how this information is then recorded within the child's learning journey
- how many observations the team caring for larger numbers of children could realistically carry out per day – for example, could you manage two two-minute observations a day?

While observation will play a large part in establishing if the children's learning is effective, a further crucial part of this process is that the adults spend time reflecting on what they have seen, ideally to include more than one member of the team working with the children.

Points for reflection

During reflection time the adults need to consider:

- what effective learning has taken place during the session/s
- identification of any significant learning or progression that has been acknowledged
- identification of any areas of a child's behaviour that cause concern
- analysing how involved and persistent children were during their play
- which of the children were believed to benefit most from the experiences
- analysing the skills the children were enhancing during the time
- where children choose to access during the session/day
- the effectiveness of areas, for example, do the children appear to choose the wide open spaces or the cosy corners or hidey holes?

It is with full appreciation of workload that I suggest reflection time and I realise that spending many hours reflecting on children's learning may, in many cases, be a luxury that few feel they can afford. However, any time at all is more beneficial than none. If we are to know our children well and are positively promoting their individual interests, then reflection provides us with meaningful information. Short observations (two minutes) on specific children are particularly valuable if they are cared for in large groups and where sections of the child's day are spent in another play area to that of their key worker.

Identify and record children's progression in learning

Case Study

Gracie is 2 years and 4 months old and is often to be found playing in the sand. She becomes very engrossed in her play but it has previously been observed that she is not tolerant of other children that approach her and becomes upset when others wish to share her workspace.

Today during her sand play she was joined by another child and did not become upset; during the children's play there were occasions when Gracie was observed to be watching other children and appeared interested in the other child's play.

Evaluation – Today Gracie appears to have moved forward developmentally and displays more of a willingness to share her workspace with another child.

Next steps: continue to observe Gracie's interactions with others – is this an isolated incident? Was it that particular child she tolerated or is she displaying more tolerance to all children?

The case study indicates that without predetermined learning outcomes Gracie is demonstrating that developmentally she is ready to move to the next steps in her play. As she grows older it is likely that she will arrive at the point where she will actively seek out friends for play, although she is appropriately, for her age, not ready for this step. However, this is a move forward.

Gracie's case study also gives an example of the importance of adult observation but, more importantly, that her step forward has been recorded and noted, whether it be on a sticky note, anecdotal sheet or back of an envelope (more detailed examples of recording methods can be found in Skilton and Foreman, 2008). Often when we observe babies and children we may begin to ask questions about what we are witnessing rather than necessarily decide what we have seen; for example, is it one child that Gracie is tolerant of, or others as well?

Schemas

Raising questions during observations is particularly poignant if we witness behaviour that demonstrates a possible schematic development of children. Schematic development is explained by Bruce (2004: 65) as the 'study of the biologically determined patterns in the way children behave'. They may account for a child behaving the way they do and can give us an insight into needs and interests. Although I do not believe that they should be used to entirely govern our whole practice it would be imprudent not to acknowledge the role observational prompts have in a child's learning and development.

Planning our environment will become more effective if we truly know our children well, know their interests, needs and genuinely know their current stages of development. The constant use of skilful assessment will provide an effective, realistic picture of the babies and children in your care; your increased reflection will result in you questioning what is best for your children, thus increasing your knowledge. Asking questions of what you see children doing, how they access resources, their preferences, helps the child's main carers to form a big picture of their development and learning; this information will combine to establish the basics of an individual learning journey.

Despite quality being difficult to measure, one management tool often used for evaluating success is that the reputation is sound and occupancy levels high. This measure of success is, however, superficial and we can never completely be sure of the quality of our service unless we involve all the users; in other words we need to seek the views, the service, parents, children and other stakeholders as required. When gathering this information, a primary consideration must be that every individual's opinion and contribution is valued and that all stakeholders are offered the opportunity to contribute, not just a chosen few who will give you the answers that you want.

Gathering information

Questionnaires

Questionnaires are a widely used method of gathering information in many quality evaluations and management strategies across industry. Before devising your questionnaire, consider:

- who is going to be asked to complete the questionnaires?
- who, within your team, is going to organize their distribution and collection?

- what length of time is to be allocated for contributors to return completed questionnaires?
- are you going to offer contributors an opportunity to return completed questionnaires with anonymity?

Devising a questionnaire may not be as easy as it may first seem and when so doing it is important to ensure that the questions are relevant and precise. They need to be quick to complete and easy to follow, but also consider providing space for an optional, more lengthy, opinion.

Interviews

Interviews are also a widely used form of data collection and can be a very effective method to gather a more detailed response than a questionnaire. A few considerations before embarking on interviews are:

- preparing the interview questions in advance and possibly sharing them with the person before the interview takes place
- the person conducting the interview is respectful of the answers given
- participants are advised how long the interview is expected to take
- a mutually convenient time in an appropriate quiet space is set aside for the interview.

If you are inexperienced in devising questionnaires and interviews Bell (2005) not only provides sound advice but also details the advantages and disadvantages of the process.

GROUP TASK

Devise a series of questions for interviews that would be appropriate to ask the children in your setting. Think about how you might ask the children, if they enjoy coming to your setting, how they feel they are treated by staff and children, and if they are happy while with you. Think about how and when the children will be asked.

The processes for gathering various data bring about ethical considerations, so when asking people to contribute it is vital that you ensure:

- all participants are willing to participate and not coerced;
- all participants are offered the right to withdraw from the study;
- answers are treated with confidentiality and respect;
- participants are made fully aware of what the data are being gathered for, who will see the data and what the data will be used for in the future;
- consider that your participants may not be confident in literacy and numeracy skills and that you do not put instant demands on people for a written response.

The Reggio Emilia philosophy suggests that the first educators of children are the parents (the second and third being the teacher and the environment). The beginning of a child's learning journey documentation will be to ask for information from parents about their home life. Many will have the opportunity to visit the child's home before they commence at the setting. In most cases this time will be spent with the practitioner asking the parents questions about the child's preferences, routines and specific needs. The advantages of home visiting can be that;

- parents are more relaxed and open in their own habitat;
- the child perceives that the visiting adult is welcomed to their home, thus receiving a positive message of trust and support which will, in turn, aid the settling in process;
- the practitioner develops a more in-depth knowledge of the child's environment and family.

If you are unable to offer home visits then the importance of spending time with parents, particularly during the settling in process, is imperative. Bruce (1997: 196) refers to parental involvement as 'A two-way process, and just as early childhood practitioners will need to inform parents about their observations of children, and plans for working with them, so parents will need to feel comfortable in sharing their knowledge of their children with staff, carers and childminders'.

Even though practitioners may be very welcoming to parents and carers and provide opportunities to share information, exchanges may happen only once or twice a year. The opportunity of sharing is a very valuable contribution to the child's learning journey so for those caring for young babies and toddlers, where rapid developmental changes occur, an ongoing dialect with the child's parents is important.

GROUP TASK

Consider your current practice for sharing information with parents of young babies and toddlers. How effective do you feel this process is? How frequently is there an opportunity to review their baby's development? Do you genuinely believe that the partnership with parents is truly a partnership or does either 'partner' have more of a say?

Consider strategies to increase the genuine partnership between home and setting to offer a true ongoing two-way communication by regular use of questionnaires or a diary system that passes between you and home.

Consider the information you want parents to share with you about the child's interests and the discoveries they have made as well as noting developmental milestones.

Most relationships are developed with time and trust, and the more effort each person puts in to building the partnership, the more relaxed, open and confident each person is in this situation. When I worked in day care I became aware that occasionally parents 'didn't like to make a fuss' and would put up with minor niggles. I always tried to encourage these minor niggles to be addressed, they would grow into larger issues if not discussed openly and frankly.

Managing self-evaluation

Many countries' early years settings are required to be inspected as part of provision of care and education for babies and young children. In England settings are inspected by the Office for Standards in Education, who request that completion of a 'self-evaluation' form be part of their inspection process (see Chapter 5). It has been my experience that many practitioners lack confidence in this, asking 'How do we know what we don't know? This question is impossible to answer as we all 'don't know' different things. We can go some way to reducing the 'don't knows' by professionally developing each member of the team. Staff training and ongoing support will play a vital role in professional development and will go some way to limit the 'don't knows' and draw on the strengths of what colleagues do know. Many will have access to short training courses that are designed to enhance practice, providing that attendees are given the opportunity to cascade the information gained and develop practice as a result of enhanced knowledge. This, in turn, will impact on staff motivation as they will feel empowered to change facets that are not working as well as they could. Changes will become part of a system that moves forward and adapts to the babies and children.

There is a risk that the genuine and worthy reason for self-evaluation is overshadowed by evaluating simply as a means to gather evidence to present when externally inspected. Part of the process of appropriate handling of any form of data gathering is to remind those involved that the reason they are doing it is to improve the outcomes for the children.

Managing a process for self-evaluation is a sensitive operation. If team leaders handle this inappropriately it may have the effect of demotivating colleagues, children, parents and other stakeholders. Before embarking on self-evaluation it is crucial that management has the full support of the whole team in advance and that everyone, at every level, is prepared to receive feedback that may be critical of existing practices.

It must be reinforced that self-evaluation be continuous, realistic but effective and that a successful team will never feel that it has reached the top because a need to change will inevitably occur along the way. Establishing the philosophy of evaluation will encourage each and everyone to question whether children are being well cared for and educated in a setting where the best service that you can provide is offered – are they happy, achieving and do they have high self-esteem (that is, the children and the adults)?

A thorough process for self-evaluation should also bring about time for the team to reflect and acknowledge its own learning journey and development, with celebrations built in along the way. An effective self-evaluation process will incorporate a system for staff appraisal that includes all the team members. This system for appraisal should be a two-way process between staff and management, and include an opportunity for team members to identify their own training needs.

There may be a temptation for some to measure success against occupancy levels and financial success. The ability to meet local demands is important, but to offer an early years service with experts who are motivated to enhance the development and learning and improve the outcomes for the children in our care will have a greater impact within the community.

Evaluating your service effectively will bring about many positive qualities that include:

- a genuine knowledge of how best to meet the needs of your children
- staff team members who are reflective in their practice and are confident to question what they see
- a team that includes all stakeholders feeling valued for their contributions
- a method of promoting parental involvement in a continual, practical and informative way
- a management team that can be confident that the service offered is of the highest quality it is able to provide.

Further reading

Laar, B. (1997) *Guide to Surviving School Inspection.* Oxford: Butterworth-Heinemann.
Pascal, C. and Bertram A. (1997) *Effective Early Learning: Case Studies in Improvement.* London: Paul Chapman Publishing.
Qualifications and Curriculum Authority (QCA) (2003) *Foundation Stage Profile Handbook.* Ref: QCA/03/1006. QCA. London: QCA.

Useful websites

www.ofsted.gov.uk

SECTION 3
EFFECTIVE LEADERSHIP AND MANAGEMENT

SECTION 3

Effective Leadership and Management

Leadership and management are two notions that are often used interchangeably. Certainly a good leader recognizes the need to manage, but leaders are also expected to be inspirational. Leaders provide environments in which staff can access opportunities to learn and develop in self-directed ways. In addition, they focus on process measures as well as outcome measures. The main aim of a manager is to maximize the output of the organization through directing people and resources in a group according to principles or values that have already been established, while leaders set a new direction or vision for the organization to follow. However, leadership is one of the assets that a successful manager must possess. The way that leaders see themselves and external influences will shape the way that they carry out their role, particularly when it comes to the management of change, as we see in the chapters in this section.

To gain an understanding of where we are in developing successful learning environments for young children, a look at the historical and cultural context can provide an insight into how we have arrived at where we are today – and this is how Chapter 7 opens.

Leaders need to understand the economic climate and have good business sense, as well as interpersonal skills, in order to establish the high-quality provision that is being demanded by parents. Our first case study in this section identifies the need for good project management skills because, as part of her leadership role, the head teacher is asked to develop a children's centre. So we learn that part of leadership is to provide vision and part of management is to provide direction and resources for staff to achieve that vision. In this particular example, the need for a smooth transition was important. The head teacher therefore took on the major aspects of informing transitions such as clear communication, developing positive relationships, supporting participants' emotional well-being and helping them to feel that they belonged to a community, as well as considering curriculum continuity (Fabian, 2007). Staff development was central to a successful outcome – not just individual training, but joint training and the involvement of parents in the development and evaluation of the project.

The start of nursery education has been perceived as one of the major challenges of early childhood – how much more so then for children coming to the UK from another country and culture? If it is to be successful then it needs to be managed by a process of co-construction and participation between the nursery and the family, both communicating and working together for the benefit of the child. In the second case study we see how important it is to use observation skills to identify and follow the child's interests in order to enable that transition. The chapter goes on to describe an example from Germany and invites readers to make a comparison between the management styles outlined in the chapter.

In Section 4 we look at ways to develop effective relationships *within* the team, but here, in Chapter 8, we are concerned with the effective leadership *of* teams. The diversity of teams means that the leader must help individuals identify their strengths through self-evaluation and then work with them to ensure that these are used within the team in a way that optimizes the children's quality of learning and experience.

Well-being, a good knowledge base and confidence are all key to the way teams work successfully, so these areas are addressed by touching on a number of issues such as appraisal, inspection and staff development. Through a case study in which a manager reflects on her own learning journey, we see how improved practice can be brought about through staff motivation, commitment and the manager's own professional development. This case study demonstrates that effective leaders are knowledgeable and enthusiastic, and have the confidence in their own abilities as a manager to bring about successful change.

Working in teams often enables distributed leadership and sharing of roles by recognizing the strengths and talents of others and then delegating responsibilities. However, the manager also requires appropriate networks beyond the setting for their own support if they are to flourish, so the manager's well-being is also an area that is addressed in this chapter.

Our final chapter in this section (Chapter 9) focuses on the cross-section of agencies that contribute to the development and learning of young children and the benefits to the whole family which come about when organizations work together. Young children need an environment that will protect their safety and provide inclusive activities for everyone. A brief exploration of the history leading up to the introduction of the *Every Child Matters* Green Paper outlines why child protection and safeguarding children is now an important topic when considering the needs of young children.

The benefits and barriers to multi-agency working and how these can be overcome are then addressed. Children's centres and family centres are designed to be a central part of the community, providing pre-school care and education for children under 5, supporting the family with training courses for parents and carers and providing activities for the whole family. The case studies in this chapter not only look at the support that these centres offer, but also the way in which partnerships between the various agencies work and how it is not always an easy process.

Historically, different agencies have not always worked in partnership, but worked independently with little or no communication between them. The introduction of the Every Child Matters framework means that communication within and between organizations now has to take place. Examples are included such as children's centres having a co-ordinator who has the responsibility of developing multi-agency, partnership working; the Common Assessment Framework promoting partnership working, and so on. Working with others brings about complex management issues which require proactive leaders and managers who can initiate, develop and maintain partnerships with other agencies.

If settings are to meet all of the criteria for an 'enriched environment' and work with a range of agencies to bring about success for every child, it is down to the staff team. However, it is the leader who must have the vision of where they are going and the management skills to be able to guide the staff in the right direction.

7

Developing and Sustaining a Successful Learning Environment

Lynn Beckett

CHAPTER OBJECTIVES

This chapter discusses:

- **Leadership within the wider context.**
- **How an effective leader can work with the team to establish a successful learning environment for babies and young children.**
- **What processes need to be in place to ensure this high-quality atmosphere will be sustained.**

In today's economic climate, women are encouraged to return to the workplace both to contribute to the economy and as a means of tackling child poverty. For parents living in areas of high disadvantage, good quality integrated early years education and childcare provision are seen as essential to improving the life chances of children. While in the rest of Europe childcare has long been established as a key factor in economic growth, England has lagged behind. The Blair government in its 1997 manifesto, pledged to support parents in balancing work and family life. The National Childcare Strategy (DfES, 1998) was developed in part to meet this pledge.

The key points of the strategy are:

- quality of childcare
- affordability of childcare

- diversity of provision
- accessibility of childcare
- partnership working.

The major challenge of the strategy was to get childcare right for all children and to give parents genuine choices. In order to meet this challenge over the past 10 years there has been a substantial investment in provision for young children. This has included free part-time nursery places for 3- and 4-year-olds, building on local Sure Start programmes in the most disadvantaged communities, and the development of over 3,000 children's centres offering integrated services for children under the age of 5 years and their families (DCSF, 2008).

These developments are central to the Every Child Matters: Change for Children agenda and are underpinned by the Children Act 2004 and the Childcare Act 2006 (McAuliffe et al., 2006).

The development of children's centres that provide integrated care and education, has meant that the care of very young children has come into the domain of a range of professionals who have neither the relevant qualifications or experience of providing day care for children under the age of 3.

The provision of childcare for very young children has been put into the public domain by current government policy. The emphasis on effective leadership has stimulated discussions on integrated centres and how the reality of service delivery has to be balanced against political strategy and culture.

Government policies that are based on a capitalist economy are dependent on women entering or returning to the workforce. Rising house prices and the decrease in social housing in England has led to more parents needing two incomes in order to pay mortgages. The rise in numbers of lone parents and teenage parents means that in order to lift children out of poverty, parents need to work.

The lack of suitable, high-quality childcare places has resulted in substantial investment to encourage providers to set up in areas of high disadvantage. In the long term, if parents choose not to return to work or prefer to use informal childcare (grandparents, partners, friends or other family members) the sustainability of this provision is going to be constantly under threat. Sustainability issues also affect quality in relation to recruitment and retention of staff, investment in resources and the development of services. Therefore an effective leader needs to understand the economic climate and have good business acumen, as well as people skills, in order to establish high-quality provision that parents will want to access. Free part-time nursery places can help parents to access and understand early education; however, they have not been available until after the child's third birthday and do not meet the needs of working parents, specifically those returning from maternity leave. This has led to the rise in provision for 0–3-year-olds within day-care settings and in home-based care, with childminders. The Every Child Matters agenda provides a framework for professionals to work together to ensure the needs of the child are the focus of service delivery and that services are holistic and integrated, not insular and fragmented. In order for this to happen, leaders of these services need to be clear themselves of their role in this framework and to make it clear, not only to their team but to other professionals, what processes need to be in place. This understanding and ownership of individual, as well as team, roles and responsibilities, contributes to achieving and sustaining high-quality, successful care and learning environments.

Case Study

The head teacher of a primary school, situated in an area of high disadvantage, was approached to lead on the development of a children's centre. The head teacher admits that she did not really know what it would entail. The area is densely populated, with high levels of deprivation, a large Bangladeshi community and children with a wide range of special educational needs. When questions were asked about what additional services and activities the school were delivering, it became clear there was already a high level of community involvement. The initiatives included a community library and literacy and numeracy projects, which have all been very successful. To quote one child's thoughts 'Why mummy no do this before?'

Although the head teacher had a proven track record in headship over a five-year period and considered herself an effective leader, the development of the centre was to throw up more challenges than anticipated. However, she did not want to deny the community better services and took responsibility for developing the children's centre, overseeing the further development and continuity of inter-agency working.

GROUP TASK

How would you establish or extend community involvement?

DISCUSSION POINT

- How would local families know what services where available?
- How would you gain full knowledge of the family, including cultural and language needs?
- How would you develop parental involvement, including those parents who are working?
- Consider support for transition both from home to the centre and on to school.

The school was newly built under the Private Finance Initiative (PFI) and there was no room on the school site to add further buildings. The head teacher identified an adjacent site, which provided immediate connections with other community resources. The experience of managing a PFI project provided another aspect to effective leadership – project management.

Staffing and management of the centre seemed to naturally fit into the role of the special educational needs co-ordinator (SENCO)/inclusion lead in school as an extension of inclusion in the community. The vision was to make a difference, building on existing connections, and to have a positive attitude to the expansion of services – daycare and outreach. It was important that the nursery provision was a seamless birth to 7 years transition.

GROUP TASK

Consider some of the difficulties for those with leadership and management roles. Focus specifically on the growing complexity of this role as individuals try to support integrated care and education in a cohesive way without causing conflict in the management of their existing responsibilities.

DISCUSSION POINT

- What training and support would staff need to deliver on the agenda?
- Are head teachers and other teachers best placed to lead on the development of integrated care and education?
- What do you consider to be the advantages and disadvantages of developing day care provision on school sites for very young children?
- How can the leader and manager, who are both qualified teachers, establish an effective team, with no experience of providing childcare for children under 3 years of age?

It was important that all staff contributed to the vision. There was already a natural dialogue with the community through an open, transparent management style. Parents were consulted through progress meetings when developing the centre. As well as the mapping out of services the head teacher and manager were involved with the management of the build phase, and the design of the building. The physical structure of the centre was based on the needs of the community, and the service structures evolved, building on previous links. Partnership working as a strategic overview was often delayed; however, operationally, personal contacts enabled communication and links to progress.

Recruitment of staff was based on 'growing' their own staff and, therefore, the team. This was achieved through joint training and sharing of expertise across sectors. It was understood and expected that staff would extend their expertise, both those from a care background into education and those from education into care, through a reciprocal learning journey. The process was to focus on day care first then outreach. In order to cover the extended day, new conditions of service had to be decided for staff being employed for the day-care element. When bringing staff together, 'language' was identified as an issue across phases and disciplines.

The manager has undertaken the National Professional Qualification for Integrated Centre Leaders (NPQICL). A main focus of this has been the sharing of languages, drawing on different disciplines and creating a different 'language'. For example, the term 'supervision' has different meanings in educational establishments to a social care context. This sharing of languages broadens the knowledge base, invents new language, by choosing what to call services, rooms and staff functions, as well as sharing the philosophy of education in the centre, cross-checking with staff and the community.

A vision of the future learning environment had to be shaped and ownership given to staff. It needed further exploration however, as staff did not know what it would look like. To compound matters further the transition from the strategic stage to the operational stage happened very quickly, with just two days to set up and open. Operational issues were not foreseen and the manager relied heavily on the expertise of staff that had previous day-care experience.

Teachers are leaders and line managers, however, their job descriptions and pay are obviously different to those of childcare staff. There is still the commonality of accountability as council employees, however, for day-care staff, this has meant adapting to the public sector from the private sector.

GROUP TASK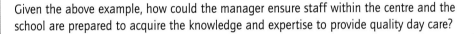

Given the above example, how could the manager ensure staff within the centre and the school are prepared to acquire the knowledge and expertise to provide quality day care?

DISCUSSION POINT

- What sort of training would staff require?
- How would the local authority support the development of integrated care and education?
- Consider the main differences between the public, private and voluntary sectors.

The process to put rhetoric into practice comprises:

1 Recruitment of staff. The day-care manager has a wide range of experience; she started her career by training as a teacher then changed to childcare, and has been working in the private sector as a manager with very high standards.
2 Teamwork – structures are put in place and expertise is valued.
3 Continuing professional development for all staff at every level.
4 Dealing quickly with staff who are underperforming. Policies and procedures are in place to provide a framework for managers and staff. Staff are supported by regular supervision and continual professional development opportunities, to include raising qualification levels, training and sharing of good practice.

How do managers know it is successful?

- Planning for the 0–3 years is robust.
- Profiles of the children show progress.
- Record-keeping is in place to support assessment and feed into the planning process.
- The atmosphere is welcoming.
- From the feedback given by staff through supervision and CPD.
- Team meetings are positive.

How are parents actively involved?

- An active induction programme.
- A welcoming, open-door policy.
- Children are settled in over two weeks.
- Two parent representatives are on the governing body.
- Parents' questionnaires are used to get feedback. Satisfaction 99 per cent.
- Robust procedures and policies are in place.

With regard to engaging with hard-to-reach families, for example refugee and asylum seekers, this has involved checking out the legal position and supporting staff training needs. There are also the emotional elements and support for staff vulnerability. There are strong connections between outreach and day-care staff training, including morale and safety issues.

Regarding the business aspects, these have involved balancing the care with the education needs of children and their families against a set budget and income targets. Therefore, budget management is key as it gives opportunities for innovation in working in this way, although budgeting constraints affect flexibility.

By developing a learning community 'together' and not imposing conditions, parents have engaged and benefited from the services available. This has been supported by:

- complaints and compliments book
- open access
- referrals – adaptation of original systems and paperwork from the Common Assessment Framework
- family files
- training courses being available
- integrated working – a social work student has helped to review and introduce new systems/ procedures.

A parent's feedback to the social work student was that 'When I speak to you I feel lighter'.

As well as the impact on parents there has been a major difference in the 3-year-olds coming into school, primarily in that they settle in well. The support for transition is key.

GROUP TASK

What processes need to be in place to ensure this high quality atmosphere will be sustained?

DISCUSSION POINT

- What constitutes quality in provision for children aged 0–3 years?
- What are the key management issues for 0–3 provisions?
- Consider the different types of provision for children 0–3 years.

Case Study

Hiran is 2 years and 6 months old and is fluent in Bengali but speaks little English. He is the youngest of three and his family have moved to England from Germany, leaving Dad behind as he is in full-time employment. Hiran is currently accessing a government funded pilot offering 7.5 hours free childcare to children living in disadvantaged areas. Before Hiran could take up his free place his mother had to register with the children's centre. The staff support parents when filling out forms, as English is sometimes limited. Children are allocated a key worker who also has an informal chat with parents about their child's routine, dietary requirements, religion and cultural beliefs.

Hiran had never accessed any other type of provision before, so nursery was a completely new experience. On his arrival he was very excited and did not know what to play with first, and would flit from one activity to another. When he realized that his mother had gone he would become upset and ask for 'du du'. His comforter was a baby bottle of milk that he called 'du du', which translated in Bengali is milk. He often held this bottle and drank from it, however as time went on he became engrossed in his play, would forget his bottle and play contentedly. Hiran is fluent in Bengali as this is his mother tongue; during his time at nursery he was able to communicate well with staff as the nursery had bilingual support within the team. Practitioners who did not speak Bengali would use English, signs, symbols and gestures to communicate with him, and that was also effective.

(Continued)

DISCUSSION POINT

What does it mean to have a sense of belonging?

Case Study

In Berlin there are a number of umbrella organizations that receive government funding to provide pre-school education/childcare. Berlin has a population of 4 million with 3,000 child-care settings and 60 umbrella providers. There are also private kindergartens that receive no state funding. The ethnic make-up includes Turkish, African and Eastern European and other European. Capacity within the centres varies from a minimum of 80 children to a maximum of 170 children at any one time. Pre-school provision is separate from education in schools. Opening times vary from 6 a.m. to 9 p.m., depending on the kindergarten. The staffing ratios are 1:6 for under 2s and 1:8 for 2 to 3-year-olds and 1:10 for 3- to 6-year-olds. These ratios are lower than in Britain and the numbers of children being catered for per centre are higher overall. This does not appear to impact on quality of care, the safety of the children or the educational experiences being offered. Staff continue throughout the centres with the child until they leave for school. This means there is a high level of continuity and consistency of care throughout the child's pre-school years. This is not the general practice in Britain, where children move through the system and staff remain working with a specific age group.

In Berlin, only 'accredited educators' or 'social pedagogues' with a university diploma are allowed to work with children – no health assistants, nurses or schoolteachers. The provider receives some funding from the state for these practitioners. These educators are able to work with children 0–3, with children 3–6 and with school children. Educators in the former German Democratic Republic specialized in one of these age groups. After reunification they had to complete an additional qualification in order to work with all three groups, even though their initial training was substantial.

The city now wants another standard to be included: they want practitioners to obtain 'Abitur' (the special German high school diploma) before starting the initial training (above). Change is already visible because those who have this diploma communicate more effectively with parents, and practitioners are more comfortable with literacy and mathematics, spelling and punctuation, and so on. There are also some students who have studied Early Childhood Education at the University of Applied Sciences. This establishment is more 'specialized' in Germany, possibly perceived as having a lower status than other universities. The first students will finish this summer (2008).

In 2009, the Berlin equivalent of OFSTED will check the quality of standards and additional services such as literacy will become the focus for this agency. In Germany there is no standardized curriculum, no national standards and a high level of risk-taking such as the height of climbing frames, lower staffing ratios, outside fires, roof gardens, steep steps, wide gaps between the climbing rungs, communal shower areas used for play by babies, and pictures of naked babies (bottoms and genitalia) on display.

GROUP TASK

Compare the leadership and management differences between the head teacher in Britain and the head of the umbrella organization in Berlin.

DISCUSSION POINT

- Consider the needs of the children and their families in both countries.
- Consider the vision for both organizations; what would be the differences and similarities?
- What are the differences in the workforce that would impact on leadership and management?

Leadership

The qualities of a good leader of a childcare centre are consistent across both countries. The difficulties of how to engage the community and the similarities of the experiences and needs of families remain constant across both countries. The issue of whether providers in Berlin or providers in England are 'better off' in terms of curriculum, quality and development, buildings, guidelines, standards and outside environments, would need to be defined by what is best practice. It is too simplistic to say that we are different countries with different histories and that answers why things are the way they are. There appears to be a paradox between the German adult culture and their children. The former is very structured and disciplined and the latter very free and flexible. In determining what leadership and management styles are best suited to individual settings, staff groups and the personalities of those in positions of authority, it may be useful to identify the key attributes of a good leader. O'Toole (1996) in reference to the biographies of the four American presidents depicted on Mount Rushmore – Washington, Jefferson, Lincoln and Roosevelt – reflects that the same vocabulary is used to describe their leadership characteristics: courage, authenticity, integrity, vision, passion, conviction and persistence. The ways in which they led were also similar: to varying degrees they listened to others, granted ample authority to their subordinates and led by example rather than power, manupulation or cohesion. They were all recognized as masterful teachers. In essence, all four were said to have inspired trust and hope in their followers, who in turn became encouraged to serve, to sacrifice, to persevere and to lead change.

Further reading

Goleman, D., Boyatzis, R., and McKee, A. (2002). *The New Leaders – Transforming the Art of Leadership into a Science of Results*. London: Little, Brown.

Useful websites

www.minedu.govt.nz

www.tsoshop.co.uk

www.jrf.org.uk/child-poverty/publications.asp

8 Leading Effective Early Years Teams

Claire Mould and Jan Foreman

CHAPTER OBJECTIVES

This chapter will:

- Explore what constitutes an effective birth to 3 team.
- Investigate the qualities needed to lead an effective birth to 3 team.
- Consider what effective leadership of birth to 3 team looks like in practice.

What constitutes an effective birth to 3 team?

There are many people who make up a team to provide education and care for young babies and children, whether it is in a home or nursery environment. Increasingly, the need to recognize the multi-agency nature of the many and varied individuals who support these children and their families is being acknowledged. As this is discussed in detail in Chapter 9, this chapter will focus predominantly on the core, regular staff that make up the provision.

Even within this core team there will be a great diversity. Each member will have travelled their own unique pathway to the position they now hold. They will be of differing ages, with differing experiences and differing childcare or teaching qualifications. What will make this varied group of people unite as a team will be through reinforcing the common ground from which they can extend together. This will involve establishing shared aims, philosophies and visions. This team practice will only become effective if this shared thinking translates to shared practice. It is the role of the team leader to ensure this happens.

The starting point of this process needs to be a shared discussion with the team exploring, both individually and as a team, the components they consider fundamental to working effectively with babies and young children.

GROUP TASK

Working independently consider:

- What components do you consider necessary to be an effective early years practitioner?
- What qualities do you possess that you feel make you an effective early years practitioner?

Working together as a whole group:

- Drawing on individual lists, compile a shared list of qualities that your team feel are key to early years practice.
- Do these varied qualities combine to make your team's practice more effective? How?
- Move your discussion on to consider what qualities your team possesses that make it effective? There should be a shared team agreement and understanding of these.

The success of this experience will depend on individuals being able to identify the talents they have and the strengths they offer. They will only feel able to share in this way if the environment is one of security and trust, within which everyone can talk openly and honestly about areas in which they perceive themselves to be successful. Effective leaders will recognize that some members of their team will need support in genuinely identifying and acknowledging the unique contribution they can make to the team. The next point of consideration must be how these individual and group talents can be embedded into high-quality practice that enriches and enhances the babies' and young children's development and learning. This process of development should begin with a reflection of the experience that has brought you to this point.

Points for reflection

Is there a culture of openness and honesty within your early years team? Do colleagues feel confident enough within this environment to discuss their potential strengths and areas in which they need support and development?

Which of the qualities that constitute an effective early years practitioner and an effective early years team are learned, or are they natural attributes? How have you nurtured and developed these qualities and grown as a team?

Having reflected upon each of these areas of individual and team strengths and developmental needs, it is necessary to link these to the strengths and developmental needs of your early years setting. This leads on to an appropriate continuing professional development programme that combines the genuine needs and interests of the individuals in your team and addresses the areas of development identified in your action plan.

The effective leadership of a developing team will involve reinforcing to colleagues that not everyone has to be good at everything but that through effective teamwork you work to combine strengths and support each other in areas of development. Aubrey (2007: 80) highlights that 'if mentoring becomes an integral part of an early childhood setting there is a genuine chance that the organisation will become a learning community and the culture will become one where learning, self-development and development of others through reflective conversations is the norm'. The contributions that individuals bring to the table can be reinforced and their value demonstrated through delegating areas of development that suit colleagues' specialisms; for example, creating specific 'areas of learning' leaders, putting someone in charge of outdoor learning or creating a position of parent partnership worker.

GROUP TASK

An activity to reinforce individuals' confidence, team dynamics and understanding of themselves and their peers as a result of contemplating colleagues' unique attributes: pass a piece of paper per person round the team; each person has to write something positive about the person whose name is on the paper; the paper is folded over to hide the comment and passed on. Only the person whose name is on the paper reads all the comments (unless of course they want to share!).

This activity can be extended through discussions reiterating that each of these identified qualities deserve equal respect, for it is the combination of these equally valued parts that will form an effective whole. Mutual respect and recognition between colleagues, in spite of role or qualification, is essential to early years teamwork. Each member has to know that their contribution, at whatever level, is important. We all like to know that we are making a difference. This is especially pertinent when working with children, as the reason many practitioners chose to come into this profession was to make a difference.

Team-building exercises can be hugely beneficial to the development of the team and promoting the ethos of working together. There is a variety of companies that specialize in such team-building days but, for those on a small budget, fun, inexpensive games can be devised that are carried out in-house. Team-building activities that other early years teams have tried include: building a pyramid using spaghetti and marshmallows, having a staff sports games day with three-legged races/wheelbarrow races, and so on, working together to make a den, and, quite simply, getting together with a pizza and bottle of wine! (Relationships within teams is expanded further in Chapter 10.)

GROUP TASK

Carry out team-building time with enjoyable activities to explore working together

As a leader there is a demand for our team to always be working to the maximum of their development. Tuckman (1965) suggests that the evolving stages a team (group of people) will pass through are 'Forming, Storming, Norming and Performing' and, as a leader, it is our aim to work towards our team 'performing' as frequently as possible. With this in mind, it is good practice to ensure that team-bonding and team-building activities become a regular part of the whole-team professional development throughout the year. Whether this takes place once a year, twice a year, or even every three months, will depend on the team and possibly the success of the previous team-building event!

Staff changes will affect the team dynamics, resulting in a reverse stage of 'forming' and therefore no longer 'performing'. It is inevitable that some staff changes will occur and returning to the beneficial 'performing' stage will be necessary. In addition to having a team-building event to support this initial bonding process, there are several considerations that can be adopted to assist the process of reforming the group. For example, provide the new person with a supportive, clear induction to the setting, and allocate to the new person an established mentor who can support the transition to the new team.

Points for Reflection

1 Are you aware of how your colleagues genuinely feel about their role within the workplace? Are others aware of how you feel about your workplace contribution?

2 Does your management structure value multi-perspectives? Do you provide opportunities for individuals to voice their opinions within a respectful, non-judgemental environment?

3 How do you manage working towards a corporate goal while retaining the unique contribution and identity of each of the individuals involved? Are you aware of what makes each of your colleagues unique?

4 Self-confidence is enriched through ongoing feedback. How do you manage the process of feedback? How do you use this process to show that you value these unique contributions?

5 Do you feel it is possible to create and maintain an exciting, motivating and inspiring work environment? Can you provide examples to support your response?

6 How are staff rewarded or treated on occasions such as planning/staff meeting? Are there special snacks and drinks to share?

7 How are successes celebrated? Are staff given genuine praise and appreciation for their efforts?

8 Consider how effectively bad practice is challenged and the process of confidentiality and respect for those who report such behaviour.

A focus on the well-being of your team

Success of the team will be greatly enhanced with clear leadership guidelines and a solid development of a job description, expectations for promotion and pay structure. Providing constructive feedback to colleagues is a fundamental component of developing an organization and must be handled carefully. It is important to remember that ongoing feedback encourages and helps direct change.

Regular, positive feedback and making a specific point of celebrating achievements towards goals will assist in a high level of well-being among teams; staff need to be rewarded for their hard work. A team that works efficiently will have a good leadership structure of support and an opportunity for regular staff appraisal. The time that elapses between these appraisals may be a few weeks to annually, but should be no longer than one year. A good appraisal system permits both parties to share the professional development of the whole team and themselves, and must not be used as an opportunity for managers to supply a list to employees of their bad points – with some positive ones thrown in for good measure. The appraisal should be a two-way process of communication with prior notice given to both parties a few days before the event, ensuring an opportunity of clarity of thought. During the appraisal it can jointly be decided on appropriate training and expectations for their role. We must remember that we are trained early years experts who work well with children when supporting their behaviour, knowing that they will thrive in an environment that sets clear, fair and positive boundaries of behaviour. A good leader will adopt the same philosophy for staff, resulting in them being secure in their roles.

Investigating the qualities needed to lead an effective birth to 3 team

The intricacies of leading a team in a way that optimizes the development and learning experienced by the children cannot be overstated. There is a need to combine a detailed knowledge of policy and practice that is underpinned with the 'people management' skills needed to nurture and support the well-being of the children, their families and the team. In addition to this a sound financial awareness, a capacity for partnership working and an aptitude for anger management (both your own and others') are also necessary requirements. It should also be acknowledged that while some managers hold or are working towards the National Professional Qualification in Integrated Centre Leadership (a postgraduate-level qualification) and/or have several years of leadership experience, there are many managers of early years teams who find themselves in the position with either little or no management or leadership training. As soon as you adopt the mantle of leader your team will expect you to be good at your job and not lack confidence or knowledge.

In addition to these internal demands there are a number of external pressures that leaders become sharply aware of once in post. It is quite possible that one of the most significant pressures is the inspection procedure that is now a requirement in many countries. Many leaders have suggested that it can be difficult to make confident judgements about appropriate practice in some circumstances and this in itself can result in you being indecisive. Your leadership role may include making decisions on policies, procedures and regulations for your setting, and these decisions can sometimes be difficult to uphold. The responsibility of caring for babies and young children should never be undermined by parents, or others, unwittingly making requests with which you find it difficult to comply. During these times our courage and convictions may be difficult to hold firm and, in order to please everyone, you may be at risk of displeasing your team by increasing their workload. It is for these reasons that the decision-making process should involve others who can contribute opinions; resulting in procedures that have been made based on expertise of knowing what is best for young children, and why.

Points for reflection

How confident do you currently feel in your leadership role?

- Do you believe that you have a clear action plan for progression and you are achieving your target or pathway?
- Do you share your vision so your team are also driven to succeed?
- Do you believe that generally you are moving forward but incidents happen that may result in a deviation from your path for a short time?
- Do you feel that you are constantly trying to 'keep your head above water' with occasions when you have the 'feeling of drowning' and that you spend most of your time fighting problems?

What does effective leadership of birth to 3 teams look like in practice?

The early years manager is the 'well-being barometer' that staff and, to an extent, parents use to assess the 'feeling' of the provision. Leaders who are confident, knowledgeable, enthusiastic and autonomous within the area in which they are leading are able to pass this confidence, knowledge, enthusiasm and autonomy on to their colleagues. Leaders who are anxious, subdued and uncertain about changes to policies and procedures will find that the broader environment is also disconcerting. The well-being, knowledge base and self-assuredness of the leaders is therefore critical to the overall implementation of development and learning within the setting.

The position of leadership can, at times, risk being very isolating, even though the staff may look to the leader as their 'quality indicator'. Effective, respected leaders will create an appropriate distance between themselves and their staff. The balance between being friendly and approachable can at times become obscure, particularly owing to the fact that most of us have a social need to be liked by our work colleagues. Although democracy and teamwork are fundamental to good practice, it is important that positions are respected and roles acknowledged. This is part of the valuing of individuals' contributions, and is as significant for the leader of the setting as it is for the other team members who work within it.

It must, however, be accepted that as a leader, no matter how good and supportive your team are, ultimately there are boundaries to the kind of support they can provide. Realistically there are, quite rightly, more times when they will make demands on you than you will on them. It is at these moments that we need to pursue and seek reassurance and comfort from those who understand the dilemmas and challenges leaders face. In the UK an increasing number of manager forums are now evolving that provide an opportunity for sharing dilemmas, issues and discussions around the process of managing a team. The forums offer an opportunity to share with those who will have empathy with these challenges plus an opportunity to increase knowledge on latest policy and procedures. If a sharing forum is not a possibility for you then making contact with other local early years managers, that is, creating your own network cluster groups, may be an option. This may simply involve you meeting with another person, in a similar position to yourself, on a regular basis to share an honest, open and confidential dialogue. An external exchange of this kind, with dependable company, will provide an opportunity to relieve some of the burdens! There is a lot to be said for the adage 'a problem shared is a problem halved'.

In addition to external support there are a number of practical ways in which you provide support for yourself. This should begin with giving you time to 'catch your breath'. Simply reviewing your current thoughts can be a productive process, especially if you begin by focusing on what you have done rather than what you have not done. There is nothing more demoralizing than a long 'to do' list with only one thing ticked off on it. Individuals are then in danger of going home focusing on what they have failed to achieve, rather than all the significant contributions that they have made to the day. How about having an 'I've done' list instead of a 'to do' list? Keeping a professional journal/log/diary can also be a very therapeutic way of evaluating significant dimensions of your leadership journey.

While it is crucial as a leader that you are aware of everything that is encompassed in the day-to-day running of your early years setting, it is also necessary to be aware of what has gone on before and where you plan to go in the future. This is an important exercise to do, not only at an organizational level, but also from a personal professional perspective.

Points for reflection

Consider your own professional journey that has led you to where you are now and the circumstances that have brought you to this point in your career.

- Think about the people that you have the greatest respect for.
- Consider the qualities that those people possess and why you respect them.
- Consider how many of these qualities you are able to apply in your current role.

Having reflected upon where you are now and the influences that have brought you to where you are it is important to contemplate your own continuing professional development. How do you see yourself moving forward?

This activity becomes even more valuable if you have a dependable critical friend to share it with. Talking through this journey will highlight just how significant your experiences to date are and help to embed the reality of development.

Change management is an inevitable part of being an early years team leader. The significance of well-being, a sound knowledge base and self-assuredness have already been cited in this chapter as providing the underpinning stability to ongoing good practice. These qualities come into their own when managing change; effective leaders are best able to respond to the change with resilience, optimism and flexibility, and these skills are only possible if the aforementioned qualities are in your leadership armoury.

Points for reflection

What do you do when you do not know what to do?

1 How do you respond to change?
2 What do you do when you come up against a problem? Do you adopt a helpless or mastery orientation?
3 Have you got a coping strategy? If so, can you describe it? If not, how do you cope?
4 What do you do when you do not know the answers? How do you deal with this in front of staff?
5 How confident do you feel to go and ask for help from outside support and agencies?

An effective team leader will observe and evaluate the impact that changes are having on their team, aware that this will have a direct impact on the babies and young children's development and learning. Sensitive and supportive interactions with colleagues are central to successful transitional development. Elsevier (2005: 63) reinforces that 'People will do as they are told – but only once. Next time you'll have to push a bit harder to get them to perform. On the other hand, if you use power properly, in an ethical way, it may seem to be harder at the beginning, but it is almost guaranteed to bring better long term results'. This is particularly pertinent when considering changes within the team. An example that, when handled appropriately passes as part of the natural development of the staff, yet when mishandled can cause serious ramifications, is the delegation of responsibilities.

A supportive leader who wishes to get the most out of the team they are working with will actively delegate responsibilities to staff. An effective leader will begin the process of delegation by communicating with the individuals involved; they will ask their team if they are happy to carry out the request. Delegation is not about offloading the jobs that you are not keen to do. It is a methodical reflection of what needs to be done and who within your team would be able to carry out the required role most appropriately. As individuals take on these enhanced positions they will require support and security, with systems established and with clear guidelines, to ensure that team members do not feel over-burdened or isolated in their new role.

It is also necessary to remember that, once an area has been delegated, the person who has taken it on will, to a certain extent, take ownership of it and might approach the task in a different way than you would have. People will use many different approaches, drawing on their different styles of learning, and as a good leader it is important you allow them to develop using their own skills and not keep control, insisting things are carried out your own way. When the balance between supportive intervention and interruption is acknowledged, productivity will increase, as will the well-being of the individuals involved, and the workload of the leader will be lightened.

Points for reflection

How confident are you to delegate roles and responsibilities to staff? Do you allow individuals freedom to make their own journey within that role?
How do you feel about ultimately having the final say on issues?

An effective leader will also be sensitive to the fact that colleagues will sometimes initiate these changes.

Points for reflection

How would/do you genuinely react when a staff member suggests a change to practice or procedure?

1 Welcome the suggestion and adopt enthusiastic support?
2 Tell the staff member that you used to do it like that a few years ago and it did not work then, so would not work now?
3 Go along with the idea but when sharing it with the team you make it sound like it was your idea?
4 Are you happy to go along with the idea but inform the team how and when it will be done?

> **Case Study**
>
> Flossie has been the manager of a privately owned, full day-care nursery for eight years. On reflection of her journey she acknowledges that there have been times when the responsibilities seemed great and would cause worry.
>
> On original take over of the nursery her main priority was to work with the team to get them on her side and be willing to develop their professional skills. In order to achieve this she gave them the immediate responsibility for choosing equipment for their children and included them in the processes for renovation of the building. After a couple of months each team member was asked about their own professional development and aspirations. Professional development was sought for all members, from some requiring basic first aid training to some expressing an interest in pursuing higher-level undergraduate programmes.
>
> This attention to the team's continuing professional development and their well-being has continued, with Flossie also paying attention to her own developmental needs – she regularly attends network cluster group meetings, the support from which she finds invaluable. The three main outcomes to emerge over the eight years as a result of this leadership style are that staff retention rates are good, the nursery has a gained a very good reputation and, most importantly, the children are happy and the quality of their development and learning is high.

Parting comments

The purpose of this chapter has been to highlight the importance of those in a position of leadership making time to reflect upon their own practice and ongoing development, and that of their team. There are so many internal/external and local/national pressures placed upon early years managers and heads on a daily basis that it is easy to adopt a reactive, fire-fighting stance in an attempt to try and keep one step ahead of the onslaught. The trouble with this approach is that while you are busy responding you risk not seeing and celebrating what is actually going on around you, acknowledging that which has gone before and brought you to this point of practice, and considering what you are going on to do as you move forward. Effective leaders will take ownership of the situation through making time to step back, draw breath and contemplate the most proactive way forward. This does not need to be an unrealistic time away from necessary duties, but simply leaving your desk and, if you are at work, spending 10 minutes playing with the children or, if you are at home, going for a brisk walk to clear your head. It is important to remind yourself continually why you came into this profession in the first place.

We can not be all things to all people, and actually trying to convince ourselves we can is not, as Moyles (2006: 30) reminds us, always the best thing for the team and the children in our care: 'Expecting perfection from oneself as a head will almost certainly lead to feelings of inadequacy: believing one is, or should be flawless may not have a positive effect on the set-ting and the quality of the childcare service. Effective leaders accept that they may not always know all the answers and that there is no shame in taking time to search for solutions. It is imperative that you do not operate in isolation; the real skill of leadership is in identifying and drawing out the grains of gold held by those around you. Rather than attempting to be a one-man band, time is better spent nurturing these talents in a way that most successfully opti-mizes their potential for the individual, the team and the children. Time should also be given to your own continuing professional development; we are all lifelong learners and must rec-ognize the positive implications of being actively engaged in this practice.

It is essential that leaders develop and thrive, not burn out. In order to sustain your effectiveness as a leader, establishing an achievable work–life balance is crucial. Just when you sigh, and with a distant look in your eye think this will never happen with your workload, remember that learning experiences do not have to come from a set text or within a formal classroom-style sit-uation. There are, of course, many beneficial leadership and management programmes available at varying levels. However, at a more informal, daily, level we must not lose sight of the fact that we learn through living life, through relaxing, playing and internalizing experiences as we live them. To reinforce the significance of this further, we ask you to reflect upon the leaders who have made the most impact on your life. Think about their virtues and what makes them stand out above others. Perhaps the memorable, inspirational characteristics they possessed did not include being at a desk, hidden behind a pile of paperwork! The question is, how will your team, parents and children remember you as a leader? And, how would you like to be remembered?

Further reading

Goleman, D. (1998) *Working with Emotional Intelligence.* New York: Bantam Books.
Handy, C. (1996) *Gods of Management: The Changing Work of Organisations.* New York: Oxford University Press.

Useful websites

www.provenmodels.com

www.infed.org.uk

9

Working in a Multi-Agency Way

Sue Ford

CHAPTER OBJECTIVES

This chapter discusses:

- Why it is now so important to work in a multi-agency way.
- The benefits and barriers to multi-agency working and how they can be overcome.
- How leaders and managers of settings can develop and maintain partnerships with other agencies.

Recent legislation in the UK dictates that everyone involved in working with children and families should work in partnership in order to provide effective support. Multi-agency working, where agencies work in partnership with parents and each other to enable all children to achieve their full potential, is identified as the way forward. This places a responsibility on all the professionals who may be working with the individual child and his or her family. A number of practitioners and agencies from across the statutory, private and voluntary sectors may be required to work together, with their parents, to fulfil the needs of the child and to ensure that the child progresses.

During the 1970s and 1980s there were a number of deaths of young children in the UK as a result of child abuse. During the 1980s the deaths of Kimberley Carlile, Jasmine Beckford and Tyra Henry were influential in the development of the Children Act 1989. More recently the death of Victoria Climbié prompted the government to set up a statutory enquiry into the events surrounding her death in order to determine whether they needed to review the statutory framework for child protection. Lord Laming's report (the Victoria Climbié inquiry) was published in 2003. The report followed a Social Services report entitled *Safeguarding Children* (Department for Education and Skills, Department of Health and Home Office, 2003) and both reports identified a number of problems within the existing system for safeguarding children. They also identified more effective ways of safeguarding children; systems where safeguarding children were 'part of a spectrum of services provided to help and support children and families' *Safeguarding Children* (p.1). In 2003 the government published a Green Paper entitled *Every Child Matters*. The green paper explained how and why the government wanted to improve the way that people, organizations and local authority departments worked together in order to ensure that children and young people are safe, healthy, happy and successful. The Green Paper introduced five outcomes for children which local authorities and organizations have to consider when providing services. These outcomes – Stay Safe, Be Healthy, Enjoy and Achieve, Make Positive Contributions and Achieve Economic Well-Being – all have to be considered when providing any service or activities for children and young people. Further to these outcomes the Green Paper advocated ways of increasing communication between agencies and for them to work in partnership as 'multi-agencies'. Further legislation such as the 2004 Children Act and 2006 Childcare Act detail the duties and responsibilities of local authorities in promoting multi-agency working. All agencies are required to share information and assessment frameworks, and to jointly plan intervention strategies and funding streams. More recently the Department for Children, Schools and Families produced the Children's Plan (DCSF, 2007a) which set out new goals for 2020 and detailed what the government intends to do, building on the results of the past 10 years. In the Foreword the Secretary of State for Children, Schools and Families writes:

> The Plan and the new Department mean that more than ever before families will be at the centre of excellent, integrated services that put their needs first, regardless of traditional institutional and professional structures … more effective links between schools, the NHS and other children's services so that together they can engage parents and tackle all the barriers to the learning, health and happiness of every child. (DCSF, 2007a: 3)

The Executive Summary continues with 'services need to be shaped by and responsive to children, young people and families, not designed around professional boundaries' (2007: 6).

The Children's Plan was produced as a result of continuous monitoring and evaluation which took place between 1997 and 2007, as well as consultation with children, young people and parents/carers. Practitioners in early years and childcare settings have built up working relationships with professionals within other sectors, that is, health, education and social services, with varying degrees of success. Prior to the actions of the newly elected Labour government in 1997, there were some childcare centres which were successfully working with other agencies, for example, the Penn Green Centre in Corby. These centres became the first 'Early Excellence Centres'. The 1999 Green Paper, *Building On Success*, launched the expansion of these centres and by 2003 there were 107 early excellence centres in the country. These centres subsequently became the first Children's Centres, as part of the *Every Child Matters* Green Paper (Her Majesty's Treasury, 2003), and a target of 3,500 children's centres across the country by 2010 beginning in the most deprived areas, was launched. These centres were to combine a number of services in each area, including family support, health, childcare and education. This is not to say that some multi-agency working did not take place prior to this; previously, partnerships had been formed between voluntary and statutory organizations, usually for the benefit of individual children and families.

Case Study

During the late 1980s and throughout the 1990s a voluntary organization – the Magic Carpet Project – provided play activities for disabled children. The project used a playbus which was adapted to make it accessible for everyone, having a stair lift from the lower to upper deck and a slide for the fire escape. In later years the bus was taken out of service and the project focused on providing inclusive play activities for disabled children by enabling them to join existing mainstream services. The project provided individual support for the children when necessary as well as individual resources that could be used in the setting. Magic Carpet Project worked with children from birth to 12 years in the north-east

Photo 9   The Magic Carpet Bus

(Continued)

(Continued)

of Birmingham and, as well as providing inclusive play opportunities for the children, it supported their families. Each family was visited prior to joining the project where the partnership between project and family began, supporting agencies were identified and contacted, and shared play/development plans were followed. Project staff attended case conferences and facilitated some families attending hospital or other appointments by transporting them in the project minibus (also accessible by means of a tail lift). The partnership working between the project, parents and professionals proved to be immensely successful for some of the children who, because of this support, were able to attend mainstream settings instead of a special pre-school or nursery. It also enabled older school-age children to attend local out-of-school activities to which they would otherwise have had no access. In addition, this also gave staff within settings increased knowledge, skills and confidence, which enabled them to welcome more children with diverse needs into their settings.

Private and voluntary childcare providers have sometimes experienced difficulties with partnership working but can often be in a prime position to support children and families as they are able to accommodate children from a very young age and may be the first people to identify when specific input is needed. One of the first settings that a family might attend is a local stay and play group; although these were often organized by parents themselves, they are now often offered as one of the services of a children's centre, either on-site or as an outreach service. In these cases they are usually managed by a childcare worker who is in an ideal position to begin to build up a relationship with the child and family. Children's centres are designed to be a central part of the community, providing a base where families with young children are able to come for advice and support as well as services and activities for the whole family. They provide pre-school care and education for children under 5, training courses for parents and carers, and fun activities for the whole family.

GROUP TASK

- Research the factors which influenced policy regarding working in a multi-agency way.
- Research your local area, identify any children's centres/services which are accessible to parents/carers and what services are offered.

Case Study

Hannah was diagnosed with a right porencephalic cyst causing left hemiplegia and West Syndrome when she was 6 months old. This resulted in Hannah having limited mobility on her left side and developmental delay. She was referred to the family centre at the local hospital where a multidisciplinary team was set up around her developmental needs. This included a teacher, nursery nurse, speech and language therapist, physiotherapist and clinical co-ordinator, who all played a vital role in supporting Hannah's development. The family felt that they were supported and actively involved in decision-making. Mum returned to work when Hannah was almost 1 year old and Hannah attended a private day nursery. Initially the nursery was unable to access direct input from the agencies involved with the family as they were based in a neighbouring borough. Instead they worked in partnership with Hannah's parents to plan for her developmental needs. The family later moved into the borough when partnership working with local services was established. Hannah is now 3 years old and participates in all the activities available at the nursery. A teacher visits home and the nursery and everyone works towards the agreed aims within her Individual Education Plan (IEP), her main target being to increase the use of her left hand. The partnership between the nursery and the local authority has supported Hannah and her parents, and will continue to do so until she leaves to attend school. The progress Hannah has made within the nursery setting has enabled her parents to apply for a place at mainstream school and they envisage no problems in achieving a place.

Case Study

Within the same local authority at another nursery, but part of the same company, the staff have difficulty in working with other statutory agencies. There are five nurseries in this local chain, the owner having a commitment to providing quality childcare for the children attending. The staff within the nurseries are all supported to attend training courses, both to gain qualifications and for professional development. There is joint in-house training for the staff and there is a shared vision and values. The staff at the second nursery have experienced difficulties when trying to plan for the needs of an individual child. Representatives from the local authority provide little support, and partnership working with the parent is also difficult. The staff are aware that they are unable to fulfil all the needs of the child but are receiving little support in their attempts to plan for the future.

Hannah's case study shows that partnership between agencies is beneficial to the child and family. In comparison the above case study identifies that this is not always an easy process.

Both nurseries follow the company policy on inclusion and have staff teams who are equally committed to providing a welcoming setting for all children. The nurseries are located within different areas and work alongside different local authority department personnel. These case studies highlight the need for identifying why multi-agency working can be difficult to put into practice and to find ways in which to overcome the barriers.

The Laming Report (2003) revealed that the lack of communication between agencies was a major flaw within the system, resulting in the government's commitment to multi-agency working. The legislation has been published and local authorities are aware of their responsibilities, but there are a number of barriers to overcome. Historically, different agencies have not worked in partnership; statutory services and the private and voluntary sectors have worked independently, with little or no communication between them. The exceptions to this have been with individual projects or agencies, such as the Magic Carpet Project, which were proactive in developing working relationships with other services involved with individual families. There was also a lack of communication between the statutory services with health, education and social service departments also failing to work in partnership with their colleagues. To put policy into practice is an ongoing process requiring agencies and individual practitioners to be proactive both within their specific work environment and the extended area.

Agencies, organizations or local authority departments all consist of individuals working within their own structures and with their own hierarchical systems and procedures and, even within organizations, communication can sometimes be limited and ineffective. This makes communication with other agencies and practitioners even more difficult. There are two aspects to examine:

- communication and partnership working within organizations – a responsibility of leaders and managers
- communication and partnership working with external organizations.

At this point it is also necessary to examine what we mean by 'partnership working' as there are different concepts. Frost (2005) explores different levels of partnership working and categorizes them in four stages: co-operation, collaboration, co-ordination and integration with agencies working through each process to ultimately become one organization which will enhance service delivery. Over recent years a variety of partnerships have been established, usually with a specific focus. The formation of children's centres brought together different agencies under the centre's umbrella. A variety of services from health and education including midwives, speech therapists, health visitors, teachers and careworkers work together with play workers, adult education and employment advisers to provide on-site services, advice, information and support for families. The children's centres have a co-ordinator who has the responsibility of developing multi-agency, partnership working.

Other multi-agency partnerships have sometimes been established around the specific needs of a child or family. Case conferences with a number of professionals involved with an individual child and family have existed for many years but more recently have been influenced by government initiatives such as the Common Assessment Framework (CAF). This has been introduced in England specifically to promote partnership working to support individual families facing health, housing, social needs etc. Together with the CAF a

environment within all the company nurseries. The staff are influenced by both policy and practice, newer members of staff following the example of more senior members who demonstrate inclusive practice within the nurseries. The extent of the effectiveness then becomes dependent on the extended services, with one team in a specific area demonstrating a commitment towards working in partnership and others being more reticent. If they both work for the same local authority with the same policies, taken from the same legislation, the differing responses must be due to the human factor.

As practitioners, everyone has a responsibility to work in a multi-agency way, regardless of their position within an organization or agency. The reasons for multi-agency partnership working are now well documented and established, and supported by practitioners. Professionals all agree that they need to work together to safeguard children who are at risk and avoid further situations like that of Victoria Climbié. The legislation, guidance and resources have been put into place and continue to be revised and improved. The responsibility now lies with the agencies, organizations and local authorities to put it into practice. Each of these services needs to work independently and together to move forward.

DISCUSSION POINT

- Discuss the roles and responsibilities of practitioners within your setting and local area, relating to their influence on multi-agency working.
- Discuss different styles of leadership and management and how these influence the effectiveness of the workforce.

Further reading

Siraj-Blatchford, I., Clarke, K. and Needham, M. (2007) *The Team Around the Child: Multi-agency Working in the Early Years.* Stoke-on-Trent: Trentham Books.

Useful websites

www.everychildmatters.gov.uk

www.ecm.gov.uk/informationsharing

www.ecm.gov.uk/caf

www.ecm.gov.uk/safeguarding

SECTION 4

ESTABLISHING EFFECTIVE RELATIONSHIPS

SECTION 4

Establishing Effective Relationships

The opening chapter in this section (Chapter 10) addresses establishing effective relationships with colleagues. The dynamics within any team will require a lot of consideration to ensure that there is harmony between its members. It is naive to believe that individuals who work together will automatically get on with each other. The number of variables within any early years team are so great that it is only to be expected that tensions between colleagues will arise now and again. You have a team that is made up of individuals of varying ages, with varying qualifications, expertise and experience. Add to that the fact that people will be on differing rates of pay, have differing levels of responsibility and demonstrate differing personal perceptions about commitment and motivation to work, and the potential for unrest is high. Unfortunately, even with the best will in the world, in many settings in the midst of the hustle and bustle of everyday provision the emotional well-being of the team is one of the last things to receive attention.

It is, however, fundamental to the development and learning of young children in the setting that the practitioners who spend time with them are not unhappy. This is not to say that no one will ever be a bit down-hearted and teams all have to become best friends. It is when 'off days' become the norm that things start to impact on the children.

Babies and young children are very sensitive to the well-being of those around them. There is a direct correlation between the emotional state of the adults and the children in their care. Consider the difference between a baby getting their nappy changed by a non-communicative, disgruntled practitioner who does not like to undertake personal care duties and a practitioner who is chirpy and approaches the task in a 'sing song' fashion. There is a link between children's emotional well-being and their cognitive well-being; happy teams beget happy children who are more likely to optimize their developmental potential. This sounds incredibly simplistic but as with many simplistic things they are often assigned to the category of 'that's obvious', not given much thought and, therefore, not much is done about them.

Chapter 10 focuses on the significance of the nature of the relationships colleagues develop. It outlines the fundamental importance to the children's learning experiences of staff having a high level of professional well-being. The text discusses the direct link between emotional well-being and effective interactions between staff members. Part of this consideration includes a dialogue exploring what we actually mean by the term 'effective relationships'. The remainder of the chapter, supported by case study examples, addresses the logistics of establishing effective relationships and the reality of putting these into practice.

The following chapter goes on to discuss establishing effective relationships with parents. Parents are clearly fundamental to babies and young children's lives, and therefore need to be central to any relevant discussions regarding their children. These discussions, of course, need to begin prior to the families joining the setting. There are a number of pragmatic reasons why this comprehensive dialogue needs to be established, one of the most obvious being that babies' and many young children cannot verbally communicate in precise articulate detail and rely on a number of other gestures or strategies to highlight their interests and needs. These personal statements need to be shared with the practitioners who will be caring for them as they are likely to aid the formation of an immediate bond. In order to prevent the babies and young children feeling any sense of alienation between home and their pre-school setting it is essential that this dialogue is ongoing. Chapter 11 details why it is imperative to babies' and young children's development and learning to establish positive interactions with families. The text discusses the various forms these relationships may take and provides case study examples and group tasks that reinforce how to achieve a working partnership in practice.

Chapter 12 focuses on establishing effective relationships with babies and young children. Children are social beings and thrive developmentally through positive social interactions. This chapter draws directly on some of the abundant theory that underpins the need to establish effective relationships, such as Bowlby (attachment theory), Vygotsky (zone of proximal development), Bruner (scaffolding) and Bandura (social learning theory).

Babies are born with their neurological development still continuing, and have an intrinsic motivation to gain external stimulation to nurture and extend new synapses and to reinforce these neurological connections. They require the sensitive and stimulating intervention of an adult (or someone who at least has more life experience than them; a lot can be learned from older siblings and peers!). We know that within moments of birth, babies are capable of imitation; much has been written of the experiment involving a mother or a father sticking their tongue out to their newborn who mimics this action. It is not a coincidence that even though a young baby cannot focus across a room, they are able to see an adult's face while being held in their arms (as if breastfeeding or cradled to be bottle-fed). Immediately, therefore, there is a demand for interaction, the start of establishing a means of social communication commences. It is quite incredible to consider how quickly a newly born baby can make all their needs known with facial and verbal expressions. The key to this successful communication is the fact that the two communicators genuinely know and trust each other.

With this in mind when a baby or young child comes into an early years setting for the first time, consideration must be given to getting to know them so a genuine relationship can be established. This should be through observation and discussion with both the children and their families, ranging from gaining information about anything specific that makes them sad and how they like to be comforted, to treasured toys and activities, sleep patterns or favourite things to eat and drink. It will take time and effort to establish an association that is founded on mutual respect and recognition but, ultimately, it will provide a firm foundation from which effective development and learning can extend. This chapter explores the various individuals that babies and young children encounter throughout their day and the diverse nature of these interactions. The impact of these various relationships on early years development and learning is investigated. Specific attention is given to babies and young children having a significant other in their lives and the role of the key worker.

10

Establishing Effective Relationships with Colleagues

Karen Graham

CHAPTER OBJECTIVES

- To explore ways to develop effective teams.
- To promote an understanding of communication skills and the role played by the team manager in developing relationships.
- To promote an understanding of individual responsibilities to team work.

An effective childcare team is one that works cohesively towards identified, common goals and targets while maintaining a child focus in the context of legislative standards. Given that provision for young children is rarely a lone task, childcare provision is reliant upon the ability of each individual member of staff to build effective relationships with colleagues. Yet a childcare setting relies upon more than a broad range and depth of individual skills that are brought together during group work. It is reliant upon commitment to exemplary teamwork to provide a strong foundation for quality provision.

Teamwork is the collaborative working of people that share strengths, balance weaknesses, share direction and build a vision; a staff team works inclusively and together to that end. The early years workforce shares with the majority of workplaces a range of staff whose roles, functions and responsibilities differ. Its advantage is that childcare staff often choose to work in the sector because they have natural communication skills and abilities that are aligned with the childcare role. The role of the childcarer demands that these skills are continually appraised, developed and refined for situation and purpose, through work with those that form the childcare team. That is: children, parents or carers, work colleagues and/or external partners.

High-quality childcare provision necessitates that childcare staff will work across a range of internal and external, often interdependent teams. These will include in the setting team and smaller groups within the setting such as the management team, childcare area/room teams and those brought together to perform specific tasks such as policy development. The range of teamwork a childcarer may contribute to during each shift will vary, often in breadth and depth of remit, and can include a range of team members such as those outlined above. Each team will be defined by its role, its functions and the responsibilities it undertakes to meet its delegated purpose. Whatever the purpose, working in a childcare environment requires dynamic, flexible, professional teamwork to meet the needs of individual children. In turn, it necessitates a level of efficiency that is reliant upon effective communication.

Preparation for successful teamwork builds upon effective communication competencies to include two aspects of team-building that impact upon an individual's ability to perform as a team member. These are:

1   An understanding of the overarching role of the team manager.
2   An understanding of individual responsibilities to the team.

What is a team?

The notion of a team is an abstract construct describing the interdependent nature of activity. During teamwork each member of staff works to fulfil a complementary role towards a shared outcome that would often be difficult to achieve alone. A staff team is reliant upon the commitment of each team member to contribute to the overarching professionalism of the team. This demand for commitment from individuals, that each role is fulfilled and that the functions and responsibilities of each individual role are carried out, is a feature of strong teams and team management that serves to protect the collaborative efforts of a team.

Foundations for team-building

The responsibility for establishing effective teams within settings is most frequently the role of the setting manager who is responsible for leading and promoting the vision and purpose of the setting. The primary responsibility of the manager is to provide services to children as agreed with the stakeholders. It is a role that depends upon the building of efficient and cohesive teams and is one that necessitates forethought and planning that will include decision-making about the construct of individual teams and the working conditions that are necessary to support the success of teams, such as catering for the personalities, abilities and needs of those who form them. Initial planning, preparation and development of teams will later extend to monitoring of the team during each activity. It is an important feature of management because the process of working towards a team goal in a childcare setting impacts upon children's well-being and development. It is a responsibility that requires of managers clear delineation and negotiation of responsibilities that are agreed and understood by staff. These agreed roles, functions and responsibilities of the team become a reference for team self-monitoring and review during benchmarking of activities that measure and monitor progress.

Building teams

There are many models of team building. Egolf (2001) describes a four-stage process of team-building that was initially offered as a synthesis of teamwork by Tuckman (1965). This simple model describes a process through which teams develop towards a mature level of productive functioning. The four stages are brought together in an evaluative fifth stage of the model – 'mourning' – added by Tuckman post-1965, to review teamwork outcomes. However, for the purposes of team-building the four stages remain those of:

1   **Forming**: the stage during which the team is brought together and begins to explore potential roles. It is period of familiarization with those who are forming the team and developing an understanding of the team roles, functions and responsibilities.
2   **Storming**: the stage during which unhelpful diversions and conflict may arise. It can be a challenging period that can feature negative behaviours.
3   The **norming** stage: a stage of managing and dealing with actual and potential conflict to reach a stage of productivity described as the performing stage.
4   The **performing** stage is characterized by trust and acceptance. It is the stage during which the group acts as a productive team and works together towards team goals.

At the performing stage the value of the team clearly exceeds any individual contribution. Its effectiveness is derived from individual team member contributions of skills and expertise that enhance the overall team performance.

Effective teams

Effective teams will engage in benchmarking of standards through regular individual team monitoring and review of progress. Reviews are an important extension from initial target and goal-setting, providing measurement of progress against interim targets that maintain the direction of the team as it strives to reach its goals. Review of individual and team progress can be used to identify current successes and actual and potential barriers to progress. Reviews provide an opportunity to maintain morale in an environment in which the team can reach realistic, optimum performance while adhering to standards, thus allowing the team to grow, to mature and to become efficient and effective.

An effective team is identified by characteristics that include:

- professional leadership
- cohesive, collaborative working towards a shared vision
- relaxed, professional relationships
- recognition of team strengths
- shared responsibility for building team relationships
- clear direction
- clarity in shared roles and individual responsibilities
- ability to self-monitor and evaluate progress
- clear delegation of responsibilities
- commitment to the team from all team members.

DISCUSSION POINT

Think of effective teams you know. What attributes do they possess? (Consider, among other aspects, roles within the team, abilities to make decisions, contributions of individuals and time-management.)

The management role

The strongest teams will move forward, building and sharing a vision for current and future practice together. Most importantly, they will feel that all team members are contributing to reaching the team goals (Adair, 2003). Strong teams will accept responsibility for individual roles and make a group commitment to team performance, knowing that contributions are valued and that the team is supported from within.

The features of a well-developed team include a degree of co-operative flexibility. As the team works towards its targets and goal, co-operative flexibility may result in fluidity of leadership as the focus of tasks alters and/or the direction of practice changes to meet the evolving needs of team priorities, roles, functions and responsibilities. This constantly shifting balance, in a bid to fulfil team functions and obligations, is a characteristic of effective teamwork that prioritizes targets and goals above personality, preferences and the desires of individuals. It is a characteristic of effective team relationships that helps to retain the shared focus, investment, vision and direction of the team, encouraging continued motivation, enthusiasm and engagement with team and task development.

Laying the foundations of autonomous, productive and skilful teams can free managers from the burden of constantly steering teams, and problems-solving for them. As teams develop towards independent productivity, the management role becomes that of monitor, facilitator and an additional support mechanism for team activity, should it be needed.

While the manager's role is to provide the conditions for the building of autonomous, self-directing teams, they are not required to be part of every team. They do, however, remain responsible for the team and for the actions of the team. An effective manager will serve the interests of the setting by ensuring that team roles, functions and responsibilities are carried out with a level of integrity and professionalism that has a positive impact on children and other teams in the setting. Whilst managers can guide, direct, persuade and motivate a team, the quality of teamwork and the effectiveness and efficiency of the team will always be reliant upon the combined capabilities of individuals that lead and form the team. These capabilities extend from an ability to undertake team tasks to include the ability to perform as capable and co-operative team members (Thomas, 2003).

Team leadership

Leadership of the team can be a delegated responsibility or may emerge during the forming stage of team development. Not all team members will want to lead and often leadership may vary over time. The skills and abilities of a good team leader includes, but are not limited to:

- an ability to communicate effectively
- knowledge of the role, functions and responsibilities of the team
- knowledge of the roles, functions and responsibilities of team members
- vision for reaching goals
- an ability to inspire, motivate and communicate that shared vision
- an ability to support and identify the needs of individual team members
- an ability to manage members of the team
- willingness to recognize and value the contribution of individuals
- willingness to take overall responsibility for the team
- an ability and capability to contribute to the team effort
- sharing the success of the team
- active listening
- emotional maturity.

The team leader has many attributes and will share with each team member a commitment to the team, commitment to team goals, and willingness to adapt professionally to the needs of a particular team task. Most importantly, the team leader will value the individuality of those who make up the team (Adair, 2003).

Individual responsibilities to the team

It is the responsibility of each team member to contribute to team productivity by taking each role and responsibility seriously. Working in teams and developing the behaviours and attitudes characteristic of effective teamwork, involves adapting aquired skills to promote productivity in the context of the current team. This adaptation, often refined in the storming stage of team development, is crucial to productive, team performance. There are seven key features of a productive team identified by Blanchard (2007), describing the attributes of team members that enable and improve productivity. These can be summarized as a sharing of:

1   Purpose and values – a collaborative effort to reach shared goals based upon shared values.
2   Empowerment – a shared, inclusive commitment to team direction that builds the confidence of the team.
3   Relationships and open communication – positive interaction that builds relationships.
4   Flexibility.
5   Optimal productivity – through benchmarking and target-setting.
6   Recognition and appreciation.
7   Morale – high morale that is important to maintain team vision and performance.

Development of these skills would first require that individuals become familiar with their team role, function and responsibilities in the context of the setting. Having understood what is required of them, each team member needs to reflect honestly upon their own skills and abilities and conduct a personal review of their own experience, attitudes and aptitudes. This review will enable an individual member of the team to build upon strengths and weaknesses, thus ensuring that they are in a position to fulfil their own obligations to the team without having a negative impact upon broader staff teams or being responsible for limiting the contributions of other team members.

Self-reflection is an important strategy that enables team members to approach shared responsibilities professionally. It is a useful tool that clarifies what each team member can, and is, willing to contribute to, or invest in, the team effort. During the forming stage of team – building and familiarization with roles and responsibilities of self and others, each team member has the opportunity to communicate their individual capacity to contribute to the team clearly and honestly. This honest sharing of potential input, skills sets and competencies, provides the team with an opportunity to plan steps towards processes and team outcomes based upon known capabilities to contribute to team efforts. SMART (specific and measurable, motivating, attainable, relevant, trackable and time-bound) target setting (Blanchard 2007: 150) is made easier with detailed information about potential contributions of available skill sets, knowledge and time. Importantly, it avoids what he describes as the activity trap of busy people doing little or irrelevant tasks. An individual skills-analysis and SMART target-setting provides a descriptive undertaking of how each individual will contribute to team targets and goals. In addition, it provides an opportunity to identify skill gaps and contribute to the sharing of responsibilities across the team.

An effective team member will:

• know their own strengths and weaknesses
• value the strengths of other team members
• work within the team
• commit to the team purpose
• fulfil responsibilities of their role
• understand and maintain boundaries
• support others in the team

- have a sense of responsibility to the whole team
- retain a sense of purpose and direction.

DISCUSSION POINT

Why is SMART target setting important?

An agreed remit

Individual ambitions to offer greater contributions than those sought and agreed by the team need to be carefully considered. While innovation, creativity and initiative are important and valuable qualities, it is equally important to ensure that team activity is agreed and aligned with the delegated functions, roles and responsibilities of each team member. It should always be remembered that agreed parameters of the role of the team, and individuals within it, should be respected to ensure that quality services are provided for children and families. An extension of an individual remit beyond previously agreed parameters of roles and responsibilities can enhance team effort but should always be offered with appropriate permission, with management direction and with sensitivity being afforded to other team members. A competent team member who acts professionally is always a welcome addition to the team, whereas a well-meaning, lone worker who ignores the needs, goals and aims of a cohesive team can be disruptive and damaging to the team, making the team inefficient whilst being potentially divisive.

Teams will always experience problems; there will always be periods of pressure, stress and negativity. The competencies and efficiencies of a team are measured by how these are dealt with as a whole, as the team balances individual contributions, strengths and weakness. The value of a team is in the symbiotic nature of it; the complementary method of individual working that contributes to a team's vision, its strength, its identity and its outcomes.

GROUP TASK

Examine your potential to contribute to a team. What are your potential strengths? What are your weaknesses? How can your plan for personal improvement? How can you develop and improve your skills? If you were building a team, what skills would you be looking for and why? How would you recognize an effective team?

Supporting change

Having built a team, the onus is on management commitment to ensure that the team is protected, particularly during times of change. It is an unfortunate reality in all areas of work that not all of those who form part of the team will possess the attitudes, aptitudes and

(Continued)

the competitive behaviour and its impact would reduce. Unfortunately, it did not reduce and Kate took action by speaking to Sue and by providing her with targets to help her manage her role within the team. Once other team members were aware that the issue was being dealt with they were happier and felt able to be supportive of Sue.

DISCUSSION POINT

Should Kate have acted earlier? Do you think the problem could have resolved itself, as Kate had initially thought? Why do you think staff became happier to work with Sue despite there being no indication at this point that her ability to work as part of a team would improve?

This example is indicative of the need to protect teams. It illustrates how the hard work put into building teams can be easily disrupted and can affect wider working practice. Kate had prioritized the needs of a new team member and had relied upon the strength of the team to cope with change. However, she acted when she thought the balance of team needs was under threat and when she felt the needs of the team should be prioritized. In dealing with the matter, Kate was clearly stating that damaging behaviour was unacceptable and that team needs were important. Left unchecked, the situation was becoming increasingly difficult. Once the situation had been addressed, the team felt supported and in turn increased the support they had offered Sue.

Further reading

Belbin, M. (1993) *Team roles at work.* Oxford: Heinemann.

Cole, G.A. (2004) *Management Theory and Practice.* London: G. Lyons.

Howard, J.M. (1996) *Team Management: Creating Systems and Skills for a Team-Based Organization, A Workbook for Team Leaders and Members.* San Francisco, CA: Jossey-Bass.

Leigh, A. and Maynard, M. (2002) *Leading your Team.* 2nd edn. London: Nicholas Brealey.

Owen, J. (2005) *How to Lead.* Harlow: Pearson Education.

Rickards, T. and Moger, S. (1999) *Handbook for Creative Team Leaders.* Aldershot: Gower.

Sloane, P. (2007) *The Innovative Leader: How to Inspire your Team and Drive Creatively.* London: Kogan Page.

Useful website

www.childcarechoices.n-i.nhs.uk/index.html

Establishing Effective Relationships with Parents

Jillian Woodcock and Karen Southern

CHAPTER OBJECTIVES

- To explore the term 'relationship', in the context of working with children and families.
- To examine the fundamental elements for developing relationships.
- To discuss the roles of parents/carers and practitioners in the process of developing and maintaining relationships.

For some time now there has been an increased recognition that practitioners and parents/carers should be working in partnership for the good of the child and the family unit. Marrow and Malin (2004) remind us that initiatives such as Sure Start and the Foundation Stage acknowledge this. The addition of more recent legislation, such as the Every Child Matters framework, Birth To Three Matters and Flying Start (Wales) only serve to underline the significance this aspect of early childhood practice still commands. Government emphasis on partnerships reinforces their importance as potential ways of developing joint working practices.

This continued recognition of the need to establish and maintain healthy relationships between those whose words, thoughts and actions can determine the quality of a young child's life is still welcomed. One has only to look beyond the 'idealism' of it and realize that such a partnership, if indeed that is what one may call it, demands a high degree of physical and emotional energy along with a belief in the rewards it provides and the sincere acknowledgement of the need for it. The process involved can be uplifting, but also, on occasions, it may be fraught with tension. It is during these problematic times that all those involved need to really appreciate the fundamental importance of robust and sustainable parent/carer–practitioner relationships.

Therefore, this chapter examines the issues involved in the initial stages of such a process and also discusses why its success is imperative to the quality of babies' and young children's development and learning. It begins with the recognition of the need to clarify what is meant by the term 'relationship' and continues with an exploration of communication, which is a key element of relationships. During the course of this study the nature of the roles played by the practitioner and parent are also identified and analysed.

The development of an understanding of the operation of relationships is complex. It could be said that an examination from moment to moment is needed, but relationships can also be measured by the changes made over a period of time (Oates, 1994). Positive relationships are dependent on many elements, one of which is the quality of the interactions between the partners. These should feed positively into each person's self-esteem and in order to do so it is essential that dopamine and opioids are activated in the brain. Sunderland (2004: 24) notes that these are the chemicals that are required for 'hope, optimism, determination, and happiness' and she cites Panksepp (1998: 144) who points out that, 'without dopamine, human aspirations remain frozen, as it were, in an endless winter of discontent'. She goes on to advise that the vehicle for such activation is to 'engage in delightful interactions', and although this sounds somewhat idealistic it may simply involve the communicators allowing themselves to acknowledge the humour in a situation and to demonstrate the joy of the moment in facial expressions and laughter.

Partnership work obviously involves communication. The way humans communicate sends messages to others about their knowledge, thoughts, understanding and approachability. People draw conclusions from the images portrayed through dress, body language and facial expressions even before any verbal offerings are made but behaviour is also an influencing factor. Daly et al. (2004: 191) warn that, 'How you behave can hinder communication, as people are liable to judge you on the way you behave' and they point out that, 'there are three general categories for style of communication: aggressive; assertive; passive (submissive, non-assertive)'. It is to be hoped that those involved in discussions can adopt an assertive approach based upon openness and honesty, thus enabling the speaker to clearly and confidently communicate their opinions and needs to the listener.

In order to promote discussion or to encourage the further sharing of thoughts, feelings and information, it is necessary for the listener to demonstrate that they are actually listening. This can be done through a number of ways which include merely interjecting with a non-descript comment such as 'I see', the clarification of points or summarizing what has been heard. Sometimes what has been heard and what has been said may differ. Effective listeners are inclined to reflect to show their understanding, but Rogers (2003) alerts us to the fact that sometimes practitioners are too quick to advise and evaluate, which can disempower the speaker and if done frequently can lead to a culture of dependency. He also suggests that there is sometimes an inclination to interpret and analyse, and this can change the nature of the subject matter, which may not always be of benefit to the speaker. Supporting and placating is another strategy that Rogers says is employed and this may appear initially soothing but can be rather insulting as it makes light of the problem. Care should also be taken when questioning and probing as parents may have boundaries they do not want professionals to cross. Practitioners also need to recognize that the mode of communication used will often depend upon what is to be communicated. The development of a child under 3 is ever changing, so it is important that relationships between parents and practitioners take account of this. Some issues will need to be addressed immediately whereas others may be updated regularly via short written messages or verbal dialogue. It is always important to remember that the parent is the child's first educator, as they have first-hand knowledge and understanding of the child's routines, likes, wants and needs. Sometimes their refusal to divulge certain information may be frustrating, but their privacy should be respected as long as children are not deemed to be at risk. Whatever the mode of communication, it is essential to acknowledge that everyone is different and individual in their wants and needs; each has their own personality, expectations and limitations. Relationships need to be built around these aspects, requiring effort, plus a will to succeed, from all parties.

The term 'parent' in the twenty-first century embraces a diverse society where the historical convention of a male–female union is now only one type of relationship that can result in parenthood. Irrespective of the identity of the parent, it has to be remembered that they will all have unique personalities. Some will be confident in the company of professionals, while others remain hesitant. There may be a tendency to assume that the articulate and vocal are the more capable, but this would be an error of judgement. Effective communication is not merely focused on the level of oracy, for it involves internalizing the content of any discussion and requires the listener and speaker to act effectively as a result of it.

Miller et al. (2005: 46) remind us that 'Partnership practice tends to be formulated by professionals ... but rarely by parents themselves'. The driving force or the purpose of any coming together, will determine the shape the partnership takes and the nature of the relationship. It can be very functional and practical, and for some purposes this may suffice. However, when personal issues are involved the relationship takes on another level. It becomes a more emotional experience but it should still remain a professional one. Practitioners must remain alert to various personality types and recognize the characteristics displayed by individuals if they are to understand and support. Certain individuals will require staff to develop partnerships at a much slower pace than others. Initial contacts must be handled sensitively so a foundation of trust can provide the platform for more open dialogue. Speed does not always correlate with quality and sometimes it is the slowly built relationship which is the more sustainable, as time allows each player to learn about each other, resulting in a greater degree of understanding.

The issue of time warrants further discussion as the demands on the practitioner can be daunting and there exists a tension between that given to the parent and that to the child. One may argue that each impacts on the other, as support for either one should have positive repercussions for the other. Obvious though this may appear, it can sometimes not feel like that for those awaiting attention. Human needs sometimes take on an urgency and the deliberations, discussions and supportive activities offered to the parent are not matters that can be swiftly practised and concluded, but the eventual benefits to the child should make the waiting worthwhile. However, it should be remembered that support for parents need not be delivered in isolation to their offspring. In order to enhance the skills of the mother or the father it may be necessary for the family unit to work in conjunction with the practitioner. This is particularly so for those who find it difficult to engage in playful moments with their child. Bruce (2005: 86) points out that, 'Most adults rely on remembering their own childhood play, and passing on what they learnt about it as children to the next generation', and this may be where the problems originate. Such cases require the practitioner to model good practice and to gently involve the parents in the play scenario. This shared time is invaluable for it not only equips the adults with skills and helps them link theory to practice, but it also reinforces to the child that they are of value. However, enactment in front of others is not always easy and there has to be a strong element of trust between those participating in the exercise if it is to be fruitful for the child.

To trust in another can open the door to the sharing of concerns and perceived inadequacies. These emotions may present at the arrival of a new baby. Although the birth may bring with it joy and excitement, it may also be accompanied with some degree of trepidation. Responsibility for another person's life and well-being can strip the most confident person of their self-belief that they can actually cope. Parents speak of feeling fearful and at times isolated as they struggle to come to terms with a new aspect of their own lives. Such emotions serve to compound any sense of inadequacy. Family members can alleviate such feelings but for some there is an absence of a supportive network. It is on these occasions that parents/carers may require help from professionals as anxiety is a destructive feeling that can erode emotional and physical well-being, and needs to be handled appropriately. Some may argue that it is part of being human and that it has to be accepted. Yet, if one accepts its corrosiveness one needs to endeavour to eliminate it. The complexities of parenthood, the demands it makes and the uncertainty of outcomes, can result in an overload of concern. The opportunity to share them with an appropriately informed adult must be beneficial to both parties, as anxiety can block personal progress and impair effective parenting. This impairment may be evident in the manner in which the parent fails to interact with an older sibling. The adult's preoccupation with their concerns may result in what Sunderland (2005) refers to as an 'absence presence'. She explains that, 'being with a parent who is too often emotionally "somewhere else" can often be far more lonely and tormenting for a child than having no one there at all'. She clearly points out that real absence is far easier to manage than 'absent presence'. With this knowledge in mind the practitioner must endeavour to ensure that the child's yearning for love is addressed, as failure to do so may result in long-term emotional damage for both players. The child may spend time searching for the 'parent' s/he lost, and if the problem remains unresolved this may eventually place her/him in danger. As for the parent, it can result in an overwhelming feeling of guilt and the pain of this parenting failure can colour the joy of parenthood. Being a parent can, and often is, a joyful experience but it can also be a minefield of opportunities to immerse oneself in a pool of worry.

One possible source of concern may centre around child development. Children mature at different rates, yet adults appear to compare age with age and this can result in inappropriate expectations. Failure to reach specific milestones can see parents and child enter a period of uncertainty. But uncertainty is a mild term to use, for when one considers that this may manifest itself in the parent referring to the child as 'slow' then one recognizes that the potential for emotional harm is high. It could possibly lead to the child becoming a 'self-critic' and the rehearsal of this thinking may later lead to some degree of psychological damage.

Sunderland (2005: 45) reminds us that, 'some things said to children under the age of five are as powerful as if they were under hypnosis'. She explains that this is because the young child does not have a robust and long-standing positive image of himself on which to refute the accusations. It is therefore imperative that the practitioner acts to eradicate such negative statements by taking the time to encourage and praise the child. On the occasions when there are proven difficulties, the intervention of a professional can provide the child with specialist help. The Special Educational Needs Code of Practice as documented in the *Foundation Phase National Training Pack* for Wales (DCELLS, 2007) sets out guidance on policies and procedures aimed at enabling children with special educational needs to reach their full potential. It provides the framework which has to be followed, but the journey can sometimes be uncomfortable and, for some, threatening. It is the trusted practitioner who can guide the uncertain parent along its path, thus making the process understandable and supportive. Fortunately, as previously mentioned, there are a number of support agencies, including health visitors, who can play a major part during such episodes. The work these agencies undertake impacts positively on people's lives as their practices are underpinned by trusted and tested policies and procedures. Home-Start, established in 1973, is a prime example of this as it offers 'free emotional and practical help to any parent, with at least one child under five … [Their] volunteers represent a lifeline for many families who are finding it hard to cope' (Home-Start UK, 2003: 1). If help is to be directed towards those in need it is essential that there are such efficient systems and organizations in place, but it is the quality of the personnel who work for the various agencies which determines their level of success.

Each individual will bring to the task in hand a set of personal characteristics and skills which ultimately impact on the success of any relationship. Therefore, it is necessary to recognize the different roles which exist between the practitioner and the parent/carer. The fact that the former may have some formal qualification or training may be interpreted, by some, as a power base. Marrow and Malin (2004: 143) refer to 'relationship power' and explain that 'this is concerned with the ability to influence others'. The concept of power raises many questions and one has to ask whether the term is correct in this context. Perhaps the issue is not one of power but one of strength, and this strength may vary according to the needs of the partners and the situations being addressed. For example, when the professional/practitioner needs to obtain information about the child, it is the parent who holds 'the balance of power' as s/he has knowledge about their offspring to which the practitioner is not privy. However, it is the sharing of this information which creates a 'powerful partnership'. Documentation can provide details of significant milestones, events and experiences but it is often the 'asides' which put them into context and provide the factors which can illuminate issues. This may be particularly so for any child with additional learning needs. This exchange of information helps to paint a clear picture of the child's requirements and assists in the type, amount and speed of support.

While considering this issue of 'power' it is also necessary to pause and consider the quality of the least powerful partner's self-esteem. Hopefully, it will be robust enough to enable a degree of equality in the relationship. However, it may be that this is not the case and it could prove to be an obstacle to a full and fruitful partnership. The healing of a damaged self-esteem requires sensitivity, patience and perseverance on behalf of the support worker. Feelings of worthlessness, as explained by Sunderland (2004), can result in praise being rejected or simply devalued. As words may not suffice, actions have to demonstrate that each and every individual has an area or areas of strength that should be recognized and applauded. However, Fabian (2002: 71) reminds us that, 'the contribution may not necessarily be of equal parts as there will be an element of give and take by all concerned'. However, when parents feel valued and respected they are more inclined to recognize the value of working in harmony. Lindon and Lindon, writing in 1997, speak about a term now frequently used by politicians in the twenty-first century, namely, that of 'respect'. This one term is probably the bedrock of fruitful relationships between those whose values and whose experiences of life may be vastly different. They point out that, 'It is understandable that workers wish for appreciation of their skills, but focus must be a mutual respect of different expertise' (1997: 96). This recognition of expertise needs to be celebrated and used for the good of the child.

The practitioner should acknowledge the skills of the parent, but when considering the issue of partnerships one cannot ignore the child's relationship with his/her parents, as its quality can influence the nature of the work between the adults. Bowlby's theory of attachment acknowledges the relationship between child and mother and, although it has since been recognized that children form attachments to other significant people in their lives, it underpins the need for belonging. Entry into new settings, such as a crèche or childminding venue, can be met with hopefulness or, possibly, trepidation. Children need to develop a new sense of belonging and this can be a fearful and demanding road to travel alone. The presence of a healthy relationship between practitioner and parent can serve to merge the division between home and setting, thus ensuring that partnership, in its varied forms, is a worthwhile entity.

How children are parented determines their approach to learning and life in general. It is through observation of the parent–child interactions that knowledge can be gained about parenting styles. Gordon and Browne (2000) cite Baumrind's (1972) work which recognizes three distinctive approaches and, although it is somewhat dated, it is still of some relevance. It refers to the authoritative parent who provides clear shared boundaries and does so amid a warm and supportive atmosphere. This positive atmosphere is also seen in the permissive style of parenting but this approach lacks consistency and confused messages may be relayed to the child. The authoritarian style demands absolute compliance to the adult and lacks warmth and affection. If practitioners are to work with this triad of styles they need to guide parents into recognition of their approach to parenting sensitively and the implications of it for their child and their relationship with them. Sometimes this journey begins with the acknowledgement and later the critical analysis of the reasons why they manage the lives and behaviour of their children in such a manner. An awareness of their underlying principles and philosophy may go some way to helping them to link theory to practice. This enlightenment may be a perilous journey as personal experiences may need to be retraced, but with the support of a professional trained in counselling skills, the journey may be worth travelling for the sake of the children. According to May and Nurse (2007: 85): 'One of our responsibilities as early years' professionals is not to judge but to build trusting relationships so that we can offer advice and sensitivity when parents are struggling and are prepared to accept it.'

However, there are times when 'travelling companions' are not compatible, resulting in a lack of empathy and the eventual breakdown of the relationship. It is true that no matter how sophisticated the 'system', one cannot overcome the fact that, at times, human nature is frail, and as such, however professional one attempts to be, the bond with the parent is difficult to establish or maintain. The earlier this difficulty is addressed the better it is for all concerned, as swift recognition can lead to a change in pairing. This is a far more professional approach than constantly trying to reignite the flickering of a failed partnership. However, this ending needs to be carefully managed if it is not to become a block to future collaborative work. Harrison et al. (2003: 90) remind us that, 'endings are one of the most difficult stages of any partnership'. They advise us that, 'Because of the difficulty of endings, there is a tendency to ignore them or get them over as soon as possible. Ending processes are as complex and difficult to manage as any other around partnership, but a good ending confirms the work that has already been done and frees partners to fully join new partnerships'. However, when empathy between partners does exist it can prove to be a powerful energy source which, if carefully steered, can be used to enhance the lives of all family members.

In conclusion we refer to Harrison et al. (2003: 14) who cite White and Grove (2000) as they note that there are four elements essential within a professional partnership, these being respect, reciprocity, realism and risk-taking. It could be argued that such elements underpin all forms of collaborative practice and should shine like a beacon during the work undertaken by both parents and practitioners as they join together to enhance the quality of life for all of those touched by the need for help and encouragement.

Case Study

At the age of 21 C. relocated away from her family, and set up home in another part of the country where she married and later gave birth to a baby girl. During her pregnancy she experienced a number of health problems and required medical intervention. After the birth of her child the family moved to another county and once again new relationships had to be established. The next two years were not without problems as her little girl displayed communication problems and at times both parents expressed concerns over aspects of her behaviour. Although her new family network was able to provide support and encouragement, intervention from childcare specialists was needed during these early years of the child's life.

    C. speaks of feeling somewhat vulnerable during this period as she was not only having to adjust to a new way of life but was also coming to terms with her role as a parent, much of which was undertaken on her own due to the heavy workload of her husband. However, personal experiences during her childhood left her defensive and this took the form of an outward show of false self-esteem. Nevertheless, concerns she had about her daughter were shared with her health visitor and she regarded the relationship as productive.

(Continued)

(Continued)

Concerns over possible autism led to an appointment with a paediatrician who rejected this idea and advised her to engage in playful interactions with her child and register her with a play group. This advice was somewhat dismissed and in her genuine concern to support her child she appeared intent on acquiring a diagnostic 'label' for her.

Failure to make progress eventually saw her seek the advice of a language specialist who visited the home to meet with C. and her daughter. This was yet another professional to interact with, to explain to and to lay bare her parenting skills, even though they were thinly hidden behind a mask of competence. C. had by now really taken on the mantle of a failing mother, and advice given with the best intentions by her extended family, merely served to compound these feelings. Although this visit was a 'support giving' exercise, it also put her at risk as there existed the possibility that she could engage in further self-doubt which would damage an already fragile self-esteem. However, this was not the case. The professional came equipped not with the customary briefcase, but with a bag of toys to share with the child. Her body language and warm facial gestures spelt out that she came as an ally and not as a critic. She engaged in small talk and made positive comments about the home and the child. Time was taken to actively listen to this 'mother in need' before the conversation focused on the areas of concern. During this period the professional kept eye contact with her, only glancing away to smile at the little girl. Open questions were posed and C. was encouraged to talk about her child. This conversation took place in the conservatory and both parties were seated by each other. There was no barrier, such as a desk, and it felt more like a discussion than an interview. This was a wise practitioner who recognized that what was being said about practices was not always being actualized. However, she recognized the needs of the child and appreciated the fragility of the mother's relationship with her daughter, and through the careful choice of words and the provision of a realistic play programme, she won the trust of this mother and in turn helped the child.

The specific support for the child came from the practitioner's acknowledgement of her problems, which released the mother from the pain of self-doubt, allowing her to interact positively with her daughter. The child had previously been surrounded by an abundance of negative statements and tension, and their removal provided them both with an opportunity to begin to wallow in a sea of positivity. Coldness was replaced with warmth and the child began to acquire a joyful disposition. Her needs for a secure attachment and to feel valued had been met. It had taken time and effort by both the practitioner and the parent but the time was well spent. For this little girl this intervention may well prove to be a lifelong gift – the potential for happiness and a wonderful quality of life!

GROUP TASK

1 You are a practitioner working in a multi-agency team that provides group play opportunities for children and families. A new family joins and appears to be experiencing difficulties in establishing initial relationships with other group members. How would you approach this situation?

2 You are a practitioner working with a multi-agency team which provides group play sessions for children and their families. A new father and child join the group but appear to be having difficulties interacting with other group members. How would you approach this situation to:

- establish trust between yourself and the father and child;
- integrate them into activities; and
- make them feel comfortable within the setting?

3 A young mother presents herself as retiring and lacking in confidence. This presents itself as an obstacle to her engaging in activities outside the home. How would you develop her self-esteem to enable her to approach new situations in a more confident manner?

4 A mother and father have been advised to join the weekly drop-in sessions you hold but appear hostile to the idea and reluctant to establish positive relationships with any professionals. How do you overcome this?

As can be seen from the discussions and activities above, developing and maintaining relationships with parents/carers can be extremely rewarding for all involved, especially the children. It is not always an easy task to maintain these relationships, but the hard work and perseverance will pay off. Good luck – you can get there!

Further reading

Bruce, T. (2004) *Developing Learning in Early Childhood.* Zero to Eight Series. Paul Chapman Publishing: London.

Nurse, A.D. (ed.) (2007) *The New Early Years Professional: Dilemmas and Debates.* London: Routledge.

Useful websites

www.parentscentre.gov.uk/

www.dfes.gov.uk/

12

Establishing Effective Relationships with Babies and Young Children

Debra Wickett

CHAPTER OBJECTIVES

1 To clarify why we need to consider establishing effective relationships with babies and young children.
2 To explore how this area of development can affect the overall development of a child.
3 To investigate how early years practitioners promote effective relationships within their setting.
4 To understand the theory that underpins the importance of this area.

The early years field is an area of continuous development. We now have a far greater knowledge and understanding of how children learn and how early years settings can provide the environment, understanding, and care that will enable them to thrive and learn to their best potential. The key to a child's learning is to provide a learning environment that will allow the child to become secure and happy within the context in which they are living and developing. In an ever-changing society it is becoming routine for both parents to work and for children to be cared for in early years settings/childminders, often on a full-time basis and often attending more than one setting or childminder. There are also now many single-parent families who need full-time child care. Over the past 10 years this change in the care of babies and young children has influenced the need to explore and consider the effect this is having on children's development and learning. As a result there has been a huge increase in considering babies' and young children's needs and how best to support them. What can be clearly seen is the need to provide an enabling environment and one that aims to encourage and promote effective relationships with babies and young children.

Developing and forming a strong attachment

Try and imagine how it must feel for babies and young children when they enter a new setting for the very first time. It will be a totally new environment for them with many different sounds, smells, voices and faces. When any human is faced with a new experience, regardless of age, similar emotions are experienced. They can include anxiety, fear, apprehension and excitement or, indeed, a combination of more than one of these. This is the same for babies and young children. Consideration of Maslow's hierarchy of human needs indicates how and why practitioners should aim to provide an environment that will offer babies and young children warmth, security and a high level of care in meeting their basic needs, such as food, drink, clean and dry nappies and clean and dry clothing. According to Maslow (1954), if young children are to develop and progress in all other areas then it is critical their basic needs are met first. He suggested human needs could be based on five levels and that progression from one level to another is possible only when one's needs have been met at a lower level. The hierarchy is discussed in Chapter 1 and summarized here to remind you of the levels:

- Physiological needs – whereby basic needs such as food, rest and shelter are met.
- Safety needs – whereby imminent threat or danger is avoided and one feels sufficiently secure to explore and move on to meet other needs.
- Social, affiliation and belongingness needs – whereby one develops group identity, becomes better able to express oneself and forms enduring friendships involving empathy.
- Self-esteem needs – whereby personal autonomy is fostered along with high levels of self-respect, self-confidence and a belief in one's ability to succeed.
- Self-actualization needs – whereby personal fulfilment is achieved through expression of talents, helping others and accruing recognition and respect particularly of peers.

Maslow's theory underpins the overall aim of what early years settings should be seeking to achieve within their provision for babies and young children in their care.

The behaviour shown by the child as they first enter a new setting will usually indicate how they are reacting to their new experience; the early years practitioner should be aware of and responsive to this. This will enable them to consider how they can approach the child and make that initial interaction a positive one. It is the responsibility of the early years practitioner to make contact and reassure the child, supporting them as they become aware of their new surroundings. Generally, most settings have a 'settling in' policy in place. This policy will ensure that all staff are aware of the needs of a baby or young child when they first begin in their new environment. Some background information on the baby/young child should be available for the appointed key person, which will help during the process of the settling-in period. This first contact is critical in forming the foundation of an attachment. It is interesting to see how, when that child returns for a second visit, s/he will often seek out the person who made the original contact with them on their very first day. This confirms the importance of making that first contact a secure and positive one.

We now know how important it is for babies and young children to form secure attachments to those caring for them. This is critical if they are to develop to their full potential in all areas. Bowlby's theory of attachment outlines the need for babies and young children to form attachments to those caring for them as an instinctive biological need. Through experimentation he concluded that babies and young children who actually experienced separation anxiety could suffer major psychological trauma in childhood. Bowlby continued to suggest that such psychological trauma would have long-lasting effects on the overall development of that child. He realized that a critical time in relation to attachment formation and a child's age was from six months to three years. During that time it is critical that babies and young children experience the opportunity to develop a secure attachment with those caring for them, be it a parent or key person, if they are to develop and learn to their full and individual potential. Forming an attachment is a need just like the physical needs that are met without question. Children are spending long periods of time away from their home and parents, so it is essential that practitioners understand the importance and relevance of Bowlby's theory in relation to attachment. If this is an instinctive need within all babies and young children, then all those involved in their care and education must be aware of this and endeavour to promote the forming of an attachment with children in their care. Initially Bowlby's theory indicated a secure attachment for the child could only be possible with the child's mother, but Bowlby himself revised this theory, stating that an attachment could be formed with any primary caregiver, not only the child's natural mother as he had first proposed.

Points for reflection

Bowlby's attachment theory directly relates to the importance and relevance of the key person system. Developing strong and consistent attachments with babies and young children in your care will give them the foundation to develop a positive and effective relationship with adults. Forming attachments with adults will give babies and young children the building blocks to use these developing skills in making relationships with their peers. The key-person system, now widely used in most early years settings, is most positive in ensuring continuity in the individual care of children. When new children arrive at a setting it is important they begin the settling in process with their key person. This will also promote a positive relationship with parent/carer, as they will have the continuity of one person with whom they can talk regarding their child. Good communication between parent, child and key person will encourage a greater understanding of the child's needs in all areas of their development. This will help both the parent and key person to provide the most enabling environment and high level of care they can for the child, at home or in the setting.

Although there should be great emphasis on the key person developing a positive relationship with individual babies and young children, we should not overlook the fact that it is still important for babies and young children to know all the staff working in their setting. This will not only lead to promoting an increased feeling of security for them, but will allow all staff to know and respond appropriately to individual children's needs. This is reinforced by Vygotsky (1978) who outlines the importance of babies and young children learning within a social context, with adults supporting when they consider it necessary. Experienced practitioners should be able to understand intuitively when to intervene with children to help them and when to stand back and allow a child independence. Vygotsky also discusses how interactions between children and adults within a social context are significant to a child's cognitive development. All those working in a setting getting to know all the babies and young children is therefore fundamental in supporting and promoting good practice and creating an enabling environment.

GROUP TASK

- Think about encouraging good communication between parent, child and early years practitioner. Try and visually imagine this as a triangle whereby the three points are interlinked and should all meet to make one.
- Consider how you meet and welcome new parents, babies and young children when they enter your setting for the very first time. Remember how important it is to initiate that first contact and to make it a positive one.
- Think about what the parents' and children's first impression of you will be. Body language can say so much. Do you smile and make eye contact? Do you have a calm and warm manner? Think about your tone of voice. These points may seem incidental but are often overlooked and given no consideration at all. They are, in fact, significant in creating that positive first impression.
- These points are just as relevant to those who are already settled at the setting. Every time babies and young children enter their setting, practitioners should give this welcome to them. Are you demonstrating this kind of welcome at the beginning of each session?

Social learning

With the knowledge and understanding gained from theorists (such as Vygotsky, Bruner and Bandura) we now have the reasoning that will strengthen and reinforce the importance of promoting effective relationships within early years settings. If learning environments can promote positive social interactions and behaviour between adults and children, and this in turn encourages the same replication of positive social interactions among the children, then we are creating the most enabling environment for development and learning possible. Positive interactions with babies and young children are likely to result in their positive overall development. Practitioners should ensure that at all times they are providing an effective role model. Bandura (1977) suggests that children not only learn from direct reinforcement, but also from observing and imitating the behaviour of significant adults.

Photo 12 Warm interactions help children to settle

Therefore they will learn from your behaviour towards others. So if you are sociable and friendly and you in turn encourage and reward this sort of behaviour in others, children are more likely to learn how to behave in the same way. Children soon learn what behaviour will please or not please and, so, through this they are learning positive social skills, if, that is, they are positively modelled in the first instance by the parents and carers. Bruner (1977) suggests the idea of 'scaffolding' as a way in which parents/careers can support children with their development and learning. Through 'scaffolding', babies and young children will learn from the interaction and help they are given by an adult. As their learning is extended and they become more competent then so the 'scaffolding' can gradually be removed. Building and developing social relationships are considered central to 'scaffolding'.

Points for reflection

Always praise children when you see them display positive social behaviour; for example, happily taking turns, sharing their toys or sharing within a game, showing good manners, saying please and thank you. Children can be helpful and kind. Always give positive recognition to this behaviour. Value what the children achieve; this can be a physical action or perhaps the creation of a painting. Children need to know they are valued and what they achieve is also valued. A sharing of achievements should be encouraged within the whole group of children so that they can learn to appreciate, value and respect one another. Children will learn from each other as well as the adults in the setting. Establishing an ethos that promotes this kind of socialization must be encouraged by practitioners to all adults, whether they are staff or volunteers who spend time working within the setting. At all times practitioners must remember they are the role models. Children will naturally copy behaviour they consistently experience on a daily basis.

GROUP TASK

- Consider how effective your deployment of staff is in relation to creating opportunities for adult interaction with the children throughout all areas of learning within the setting.
- What activities and opportunities do you provide for children to interact with each other?
- How do you model good social skills and behaviour within your setting?
- In what ways can you encourage a positive approach/solution to a situation where a negative incident has occurred?
- Do you have a special time, such as circle time, when children can listen to each other and talk about feelings, friendships and social relationships?
- Intervene when necessary if adult support is needed, but do not interrupt.
- How often do you play alongside children at their level in a positive, equal way?
- Find time to observe how the children are interacting and socializing with each other.

Case Study

Sam is blond-haired, blue-eyed and 2 years and 6 months old. He bounds into pre-school every morning smiling and greeting staff in a happy and positive manner. Staff respond to this behaviour with smiles of affection and warmth. They verbally reply to his greeting by saying, 'Hello Sam. How are you today?' One of them will usually pick Sam up and give him a cuddle and then lead him to an area within the setting and play with him. Sam is happy to say goodbye to his mum, when she goes over to him to say goodbye. He settles into his morning session at pre-school well, often by this time wandering off from the member of staff who was playing with him, to explore the room and interact with other children now arriving. During the session Sam seems confident and happy, playing and socializing with the other children. He displays no signs of any behaviour that would indicate concern. He responds well when communicating with adults and he is learning the rules and boundaries of the setting in accordance with his age.

> ## 📁 Case Study
>
> Jack is 2 years and 6 months old, and he has dark brown hair and grey eyes. He walks into pre-school every morning displaying apprehensive body language. His face is without expression, no smiles. He stays very close to his mum and is reluctant to leave her side. He makes no greeting or interaction with staff and very rarely do they with him, in fact he often comes in unnoticed. He will say goodbye to his mum without any signs of separation anxiety, although he does not seem completely happy either. He wanders off to explore and to find an activity or toy to play with. At this point, often a dispute with another child will occur. This is when a member of staff who steps in to deal with the conflict then gives attention to him. Jack is finding it hard to accept the rules, routine and boundaries within the setting. He finds it difficult to sit quietly at circle time and usually displays loud behaviour at this time and tries to get up and walk around. Most days he will need adult support at circle time. During the morning he encounters several conflicts with other children. It seems he is frequently receiving negative interactions with the staff as they try to deal with his behaviour towards other children.

A summary of the two case studies

Sam seems to be settled well within the setting. There are signs of positive relationships forming between himself and staff. He seems to be able to relate well to the adults caring for him and, because he feels a sense of security with them, he is happy to separate from his mum. Sam is beginning to socialize well with the other children and through this he is starting to develop positive relationships with his peers.

Jack's behaviour would indicate he is not completely settled into the setting. Although he does not object to his mum leaving him there, and he does not show signs of acute distress, he still appears to be insecure and unable to show signs of developing positive relationships with adults or children within the setting. The interactions he has with the staff are mainly negative, owing to his behaviour. Jack is experiencing negative interactions with the adults and children, and this could be preventing him from forming positive relationships

Final thoughts on the case studies

Sam is forming positive relationships with the adults working in the setting. Because he is experiencing and learning this positive interaction it is helping him learn to relate in the same manner with his peers and, so, is helping him learn at this young age the foundation of forming effective and positive relationships with those he is socially interacting with at the same level.

Jack is unable to begin this same process as Sam, because he is not yet experiencing the forming of a positive relationship with the adults within the setting. He needs to establish this if he is to learn the foundations of forming effective and positive relationships with his peers.

Points for reflection

Observation of these two children clearly indicates how a practitioner can help Jack to share the same positive experience that Sam is already experiencing from the pre-school environment. When Sam enters pre-school every morning he is bright and cheerful and the staff automatically respond to this in a positive manner and give Sam positive attention. The manner in which Jack enters pre-school seems to go unnoticed by the staff. Practitioners must not assume just because a child does not look for attention that they do not need it. In fact, this is where intervention by staff, or to be more specific, the child's key person, is needed. It may help Jack if his key person approached him and greeted him as he entered the setting. A smiling face and someone actually noticing him and giving him attention may help Jack. The key person should initiate conversation with Jack: ask him how he is today and what would he like to do first, where would he like to play. If Jack can begin to experience the foundation of a relationship with his key person then he may be able to build on this experience and begin to use these newly acquired skills in forming relationships with his peers. His social development within the setting should then begin to develop and become more positive.

GROUP TASK

- Always remember that babies and young children are unique. Think about those in your setting. Discuss their different personalities, characters and interests. Understand how by getting to know the babies and children in your setting and valuing them as individuals this enables you to support and encourage their individual needs.
- Young children cannot always initiate conversation, they need the adult to do this first. Practitioners must have an awareness of this. Consider how you encourage conversation with the young children in your care, especially those children who have not yet developed these language skills.
- Establishing the first communication links with babies is fundamental to establishing early socialization with those in your care. How are these bonds formed in your setting?
- Observing children will help practitioners to recognize the best possible approach to a child in promoting effective relationships. Making time to stand back and observe how they are interacting and socialising within the setting will enable practitioners to do this. How do you observe the interactions and socialisation of the babies and young children in your care?

Physical development

Current research has provided underpinning knowledge needed to understand the importance of brain development in relation to babies' and young children's overall development. It is now recognized that babies' brains develop at an amazing pace during their early years. Even though a baby's brain contains approximately 100 billion neurons, the newborn brain weighs only about one-quarter as much as the adult brain. Neurons grow, and that accounts for some of the difference, but mostly what changes is the wiring. Brains are genetically wired at birth, but the complex circuitry that allows mature thought processes to occur only begins to develop in early childhood and connections continue to be made through life and are shaped by experience. Neuroscience has started to map out the ways in which young brains make the connections that are the key to each child's personality/mind. What is now evident from neuroscience is that 'normal' brain development in early childhood is dependent upon environmental input, and for parents/careers and early years practitioners this means warm and loving, appropriate interaction with babies and young children who are living and cared for in a safe context, in which they are nourished and nurtured and allowed opportunities to explore. Gopnik et al. (2001) summarize evidence from research in philosophy, psychology, neuroscience, linguistics and other disciplines to provide an account of how babies and young children learn about the world around, about people and relationships and about language, linking their discussion to what is known about brain development. They continue to suggest, through scientific study, that nature has designed adults to teach babies and young children just as much as it has designed babies and young children to learn, and that it indicates we should talk, play, laugh and interact with them, giving them attention when we are with them, often though there is simply little time for such opportunities (Gopnik et al. 2001).

Drawing on this growing wealth of research, an understanding can be gained as to why it is so important for babies and young children to experience the environmental factors previously discussed within this chapter. Realizing how rapidly the brain develops at this time completely underpins the reasoning why early years practitioners should strive to promote this environment within their settings. The time from birth to 3 years is significant in setting down the foundation for a holistic approach to human development. Bowlby (1965) refers to the ages of 6 months to 3 years as critical in having the opportunity to form strong attachments. This links fully with neurological research that outlines the critical nature of the birth to 3 years period for neural connection.

Babies and young children need loving, responsive, sensitive key people around them, people who recognize their fascination with and curiosity about what is going on in the world in which they are growing up. Opportunities need to be provided for them to explore and solve problems through active learning, they need to socialize to make friends and share experiences and yet have times when they can be encouraged to focus alone. (Sure Start, 2002)

If this approach can be offered to babies and young children at this critical period of brain development, then they will be given the best possible start.

Points for reflection

Practitioners caring for babies and young children need to have an understanding of the physical development that is occurring at this time. This will help them to appreciate the importance of the type of environment they are providing and the opportunities. It will also allow them to consider the implications to a baby or young child if this is not provided. This understanding will encourage practitioners to value the importance of their provision and to ensure all staff and volunteers share in the same ethos. A consistency throughout the setting is essential if this is to be achieved.

- Practitioners must understand the needs of the baby/young child in relation to their age and their physical development that is occurring at that time. Observations and assessments again will enable practitioners to meet physical needs appropriately and to support them in accordance with the child's age and level of development and learning.
- Consider regular evaluations of the setting's equipment and resources. As the children physically develop then the equipment and resources must remain matched to meet the needs of the children at that time. This will mean staff regularly rotating a variety of resources to provide appropriate physical learning opportunities for specific stages and level of development.
- Consideration must be given to recognition of physical developmental delays. Staff meetings should enable all staff to express and share with colleagues any concerns they may have. The more this area is discussed between you, the less chance there is of problems slipping through the net unnoticed. A greater awareness will be created among staff, which will lead to the setting seeking relevant action efficiently.

Throughout this chapter there are some key points that significantly stand out. Every baby and young child should have the right to grow up in this kind of environment. It could even be considered neglectful and an act against their human rights for them not to experience this. For all those involved in caring and educating babies and young children it should be their role and duty to provide an environment such as this. This environment is so easily achievable if all those working in this sector were educated and had an understanding of this knowledge. It is critical for a holistic approach to their development and learning that practitioners strive to give a loving, caring, secure and consistent base to build upon. They must be competent role models and, most importantly, really get to know and understand the children in their care. They need to take time to talk and to play with them, building and forming a strong relationship and bond which will enable practitioners to appreciate and value them for the special individuals that they are.

Further reading

Goldschmied, E. and Jackson, S. (2004) *People under Three, Young Children in Day Care*. 2nd edn. London and New York: Routledge.
Reddy, V. (2008) *How Infants Know Mind*. London: Harvard University Press.

Useful websites

www.communityplaythings.co.uk

www.preschool.org.uk

Conclusion

Hilary Fabian

When we set out to write this book we were aware that there would be overlap between some of the aspects, for example relationships and management, but we needed to separate them into groups for the purposes of writing. Now, in this conclusion, I can bring some of these back together again. One common thread that goes throughout the book is child development; it is the central driving force behind what we do, not just in relating to children but in managing the environment, ensuring that standards are met, working with others for the benefit of the child and in having an understanding that informs a vision to move forward with confidence. Indeed, Rebecca Morton (Chapter 4) reminds us that policy is driven by what constitutes good practice in child development. Holistic development is sometimes seen in simplistic terms and often as separate areas. Kate Wagner (Chapter 1) has demonstrated the overlap of theories but there is also a need to see development as interlocking. Gonzalez (2007: 21) has addressed this with her five balls representing different aspects of the holistic development of children:

> The blue ball is about peace, social skills, working as a team and solving conflicts. The red ball is about intellectual and cognitive development, focusing on concentration and perception. The yellow ball is about the spirit, and the focus is on self esteem and character education, helping children to respect each other and manage their anger in positive ways. The green ball represents the environment and aspects of health such as immunisations, and the black ball is all about the body's physical development.

We have seen other such divisions within the book such as the six 'areas of learning', the five 'outcomes' of Every Child Matters and indeed, the four themes into which we have divided the book. While none of these models is satisfactory, and each has its limitations, we have presented them to show the complexity, but equally, the variety of tools to help you understand practice in terms of what is best in different circumstances.

Another theme that runs throughout the book is observation. We are reminded by Jane Bulkeley (Chapter 2) that observation of children is concerned with watching, listening and gathering evidence in order to develop children's learning, understanding and experiences. These observations provide the factual evidence needed to make assessments to inform effective plans which support children's development to allow them to progress further. Getting it right early is important. We know that children from low socio-economic backgrounds do not achieve as well as those from more affluent backgrounds, that girls and boys develop at different rates, and that parents often need support. Sue Ford (Chapter 9) has shown us that working together can make a difference for all children, not just the most vulnerable in our society.

Partnership with agencies is addressed and partnership with parents is a key theme. There is a focus across much of Europe on provision for very young children, but a particular focus in the UK is on parenting and how societal changes have changed the way parents raise their children. There is an anxiety about parenting, so much so that there are government initiatives to ensure that parents are involved with their children's learning and are given the skills to support their children's development. Jill Woodcock and Karen Southern (Chapter 11) have outlined ways in which positive relationships with parents which encourage a sharing of views can support children's learning.

Respect for one another is so important in developing effective relationships, and as Debra Wickett (Chapter 12) points out, developing strong attachments with children takes time but children can, and do, form multiple attachments. Sensitivity is not the only factor in forming effective attachments, as the caregiver's own experiences as well as the social and economic environment will also influence the formation of attachments. The quality of these early attachments is likely to influence later development, subsequent relationships and children's cognitive development.

Developing a community of learners who learn from birth to the grave – the lifelong learning agenda – suggests an understanding of learning itself – but what is learning? How do children develop resilience to cope with transitions into, through and from each phase of education while negotiating learning that runs in parallel to more formal learning? What is clear, is that learning is a social process that is co-constructed in context and that learning to learn begins from the very beginning of life. By developing an appreciation of babies' and young children's behaviour, Fran Morton (Chapter 3) demonstrates how we can support learning by communicating with children and developing their interests; helping them to participate in a community where newcomers are welcomed. An environment that is caring and creative sets the foundation for children's holistic development and lifelong learning. Lynn Beckett (Chapter 7) enhances and deepens our understanding of effective learning environments by focusing on the specific interests and developmental needs of children. The environment and the ethos that is created in early years settings, as the EPPE project has identified, is a central contributor to children's development.

Skill in communication is another recurring theme and this is reiterated strongly by Karen Graham (Chapter 10) as she outlines how effective relationships between colleagues are built on open and honest dialogue. We revisit her discussion about teams with Claire Mould and Jan Foreman (Chapter 8) when we are reminded again of Tuckman's (1965) stages that an evolving team passes through. Their chapter focuses on managing relationships within groups and between management and staff to develop successful teams. When we come to leadership and management, one of the difficulties is separating the two. Sue Ford (Chapter 9) expresses this well when she suggests that management can be seen as the practical aspect, organizing things or people, while leadership is more a quality demonstrated by those who can inspire and enthuse individuals or an entire workforce.

One of the main themes throughout the book is the way in which policy informs practice. In England the introduction of the Every Child Matters framework has influenced recent legislation and policy developments, many of which, including the inspection framework, are addressed by Mike Carter (Chapter 5), with the self-evaluation element revisited by Jan Foreman (Chapter 6) when she explores issues of self-improvement.

The combination of multi-layers in each chapter is considered a strength of the book and highlights work with young children as being multi-professional and multi-voiced. This is seen in the case studies and points for discussion in each chapter, which have been included to illustrate practice and help readers to reflect on their own philosophy. If we can interrogate the derivation of our personal beliefs and evaluate our impact, perhaps we can improve our practice for the benefit of those in our care.

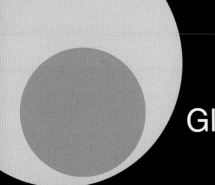

Glossary

Academic attainment   What pupils, students and children know (and can do) in terms of what they are taught (usually at school). This can be 'measured' using National Curriculum Levels or statements of capability such as the Early Learning Goals or Desirable Learning Outcomes.

Assessment   What adults do to 'measure' or estimate children's attainment.

Attachment   The bond between a child and significant other(s) in their lives.

Building Schools for the Future (BSF)   A programme of replacing school buildings to enable all English secondary schools to be replaced or renovated over the next few years. Hugely expensive, it also aims to provide buildings that suit the current and future needs of learners.

Childminder   Commonly understood as a person (or team) who cares for individual or small groups of children during periods of the day, allowing their parents to be otherwise occupied.

Children's and Young People's Plan (CYPP)   The plan that local authorities devise to improve the provision that an area makes to meet a range of needs that children and young people may have. It often involves public, private and voluntary sectors.

Children's Centres   Children's Centres provide multi-agency services that are flexible and meet the needs of young children and their families.

The Children's Plan   An overarching plan that brings together many existing initiatives, for example, Sure Start, and enhances others in a cohesive way whereby the interrelationship between them is evident.

Children's Workforce Development Council (CWDC)   An English 'quango' set up to over-see the training and improvement of the many adults that are involved in providing for the needs of young children, usually the under-5s.

Common Assessment Framework (CAF)   An English innovation that allows for reviewing of a child's overall needs within the five ECM Outcomes. The assessment may lead to local provision to help overcome a child's barrier(s) to learning and usually involves multiple services and consequently is completed online with confidentiality safeguards.

Continuing professional development (CPD)   Updating skills, training, re-training, in-service education and further development of professionals.

Criminal Records Bureau (CRB)   The body that provides checks to ascertain that adults who may be working with children have no significant criminal record. To work unsupervised with any child or children an enhanced CRB check is required.

CSSIW   Care and Social Services Directorate Wales.

Day care   It was first used to indicate that the children received no educational provision. However, it is now known that education and care are inseparable.

DCSF   Department for Children, Schools and Families in England.

Distance learning   Sometimes used as a method of providing CPD. Distance learning is where study takes place at a venue separate from its originator. Typically it would involve book learning and learning on line.

Early Years Foundation Stage (EYFS)   A legislative document which sets out the learning and development requirements that all early years providers in England have a duty to deliver.

Eco schools   A status that schools can gain at several levels, that shows they are helping to sustain the environment and their pupil's awareness is raised.

Educational provision   All that a school or setting does to meet the pupils'/children's needs. This includes the environment, what adults do and say as well as the curriculum and care.

EPPE   The Effective Provision of Pre-School Education Project. EPPE, EPPE 3–11 and EPPE 3–14 are longitudinal studies funded by the Department for Children, Schools and Families.

Evaluating   The analysis and comparison of, for example, provision in one setting/school with that of other settings/schools. It is the process of working out how good something is.

Every Child Matters (ECM)   A term coined by the English DCSF, to suggest five overarching outcomes or states that are desired for all our children and young people; for example, that they are healthy.

Extended schools   A programme of provision made at (or near) a school that usually takes place outside school curriculum time.

Family centres   Family centres are community resources providing local support to parents and children.

Foundation Phase   The term used in Wales for the phase of learning between 3 and 7 years old.

Foundation Stage   The term used by schools to discuss children younger than 5.

Foundation Stage Profile   A document used for each pupil under 5 that outlines their attainment in the EYFS, at least by the end of the Reception Year.

Healthy Schools Status   A status that schools can earn in which they have to show there is good provision to help pupils stay healthy.

Joint Area Review (JAR)   An inspection system carried out by OFSTED and the Audit Commission that evaluates the provision made through the many services in a local authority area.

Local Safeguarding Children's Board   A group set up to ensure the overall safety of children in an area. They replace 'Child Protection' teams.

Mesosystem   Bronfenbrenner's theory which links two or more microsystems together, directly or indirectly to become an interconnected set of contexts. The relationships between each of the contexts or microsystems constitute the mesosystem.
See http://pt3.nl.edu/paquetteryanwebquest.pdf.

Monitoring   Monitoring is the means by which evidence is found that will support an evaluation. This should not be confused with evaluation but it does precede it.

National Professional Qualification in Integrated Centre Leadership (NPQICL)   This is a Master's-level qualification in working in multi-agency and multidisciplinary environments across education, health and social services. The programme is specifically for leaders within multi-agency, early years settings.

Office for Standards in Education (OFSTED)   Although government funded, OFSTED is a non-government body set up to monitor and evaluate the education system and, now, all the provision made for care and education of young babies and children. It uses the services of inspectors who are trained and employed by one of five RISPs.

Parent   The term 'parent' can no longer be based on the assumption of a male–female union who are the child's natural parents. Bastiani and Doyle (1994) suggest that there are 'children in lone parent families; children who live in "reconstituted" families, with a mixture of natural and step-parents; children who are "looked after" by local authorities' (Bastiani, J. and Doyle, N. (1994) *Home and School: Building a Better Partnership*. London: National consumer Council: 20).

Personalized learning   The term used to allude to a large number of strategies that schools are increasingly using to make pupils' learning more individual and better matched to their needs.

Practitioner   The term used to broadly describe the wide range of individuals who provide care and education for babies and young children.

Reception Year   All those children who are 4 and will be 5 before or during the next school year.

Regional Inspection Service Provider (RISP)   In England five private companies have won contracts from OFSTED to inspect schools and settings, and so on, within particular areas. They do this with close oversight from OFSTED.

Safeguarding   Ensuring that children are not exposed to potentially harmful risks. The new term for child protection but with a wider connotation.

Self-evaluation   Evaluations that are carried out by the school or setting itself. This is now requested by OFSTED (not a statutory requirement) but, more importantly, provides greater focus and awareness of ways to improve. A self-evaluation form is available and can be completed online.

Setting   An all encompassing term used to refer to the varied types of provision that babies and young children experience, for example children centres, nurseries and pre-school groups could all be referred to as settings.

SMART objectives   Specific, measurable, attainable, relevant and time-bound objectives.

Sure Start   A DCFS initiative to provide better improvision for children and their families in areas of some deprivation. Specific funding is provided through local authorities that enables targeted support.

Welfare   The term generally used to indicate aspects of a child's life, mostly under the Every Child Matters headings. The term is often used to differentiate provision from educational provision.

ZPD   Zone of proximal development. A term developed by Vygotsky to describe the level of potential development that can be achieved under guidance from a more 'knowledgeable other'.

References

Section 1   Introduction

Oates, J. (2007) 'Attachment matters', *Early Childhood Matters,* November (109), Bernard Van Leer Foundation.

Simpson, D.J. (2001) 'John Dewey's Concept of the Student' in *Canadian Journal of Education,* 26(2) 183–200.

Chapter 1

Adams, D. (1998) *Dirk Gently's Holistic Detective Agency.* London: Pocket Books.

Anning, A., Cullen, J. and Fleer, M. (eds) (1994) *Early Childhood Education.* London: Sage.

Bancroft, D. and Carr, R. (eds) (1999) *Influencing Children's Development.* Milton Keynes: Open University Press.

Blenkin, G. and Kelly, A.V. (1994) *Early Childhood Education: A Developmental Curriculum.* London: Paul Chapman Publishing.

Bronfenbrenner, U. (1989) 'The ecological systems theory', in R. Vasta (ed.), *Annals of Child Development,* (6) pp. 87–250. Cambridge, MA: Harvard University Press.

Bruce, T. (2004) *Early Childhood Education.* 3rd edn. London: Hodder Arnold.

Christie, F. (1997) 'Curriculum macrogenres as forms of initiation into a culture', in F. Christie and J.R. Marten (eds), *Genre and Institutions: Social Processes in the Workplace and School.* London: Continuum International Publishing Group. pp. 134–45.

Daly, M., Byers, E. and Taylor, W. (2004) *Early Years Management in Practice.* Oxford: Heinemann Educational.

Department for Education and Skills (DfES) (2007) *The Statutory Framework for the Early Years Foundation Stage.* London: DfES Publications.

Devereux, J. (1997) 'What you see depends on what we look for: observation as part of teaching and learning in the early years', in S. Robson and S. Smedley (eds), *Education in Early Childhood First Things First.* London: David Fulton. pp. 75–86.

Effective Provision of Pre-school Education Project (EPPE) (2003) *The Effective Provision of Pre-school Education Project: Findings from Pre-School Period.* www.ioe.ac.uk (accessed 14 March 2008).

Erikson Institute (2008) www.erikson.edu (accessed 14 March 2008).

Every Child Matters (2008) www.everychildmatters.gov.uk (accessed 13 March 2008).

Flanagan, C. (2004) *Applying Psychology to Early Child Development.* London: Hodder and Stoughton.

Froebel Web (2008) www.froebelweb.org (accessed 14 March 2008).

Giddens, A. (2006) *Sociology.* London: Polity Press.

Gross, R. (2002) *Psychology: The Science of Mind and Behaviour.* 4th edn. London: Hodder and Stoughton.

Gupta, P. and Richardson, K. (1995) 'Theories of cognitive development', in V. Lee and P. Gupta (eds), *Children's Cognitive and Language Development.* Milton Keynes: Open University Press. pp. 1–44.

Haralambos, M., Heald, R.M. and Holborn, M. (eds) (2004) *Sociology: Themes and Perspectives.* London: Collins Educational.

Hayes, N. (1994) *Foundation of Psychology.* 2nd edn. London: Routledge.

Jones, B.L. (2004) 'Play in early childhood', in T. Maynard and N. Thomas (eds), *An Introduction to Early Childhood Studies.* London: Sage. pp. 192–204.

Karpov, Y. (2005) *The Neo-Vygotskian Approach to Child Development.* Cambridge: Cambridge University Press.

Katz, L. (1995) *How Can We Strengthen Children's Self-esteem?* www.kidsource.com (accessed 21 November 2007).

Katz, L. (1997) *Child Development Knowledge and Teachers of Young Children.*www.ceep.crc.uiuc.edu/eearchive/books/childdev.html (accessed 14 March 2008).

Maslow, A. (1943) 'A theory of human motivation', *Psychological Review,* 50(4): 370–96.

MacNaughton, G. (2005) *Doing Foucault in Early Childhood Studies.* Abingdon: Routledge.

McNaughton, G. (2003) *Shaping Early Childhood.* Buckingham: Open University Press.

Ministry of Education (1996) *Early Childhood Curriculum.* www. minedu.govt.nz.

Ministry of Social Affairs and Health (2003) National Curriculum Guidance on ECEC in Finland. www.varttua.states.fi.

Palmer, S. and Dolya, G. (2004) 'Freedom of thought', *Times Educational Supplement,* 30 July: 16.

Piaget, J. (1929) *The Child's Conception of the World.* London: Routledge and Kegan Paul.

Riley, J. (ed.) (2007) *Learning in the Early Years 3–7.* 2nd edn. London: Sage.

Rinaldi, C. (2006) *In Dialogues with Reggio Emilia: Listening, Researching and Learning.* London: Routledge.

Rose, N. (1999) *Governing the Soul – the Shaping of the Private Self.* London: Routledge.

Russell, B. (1994) *On Education, Especially in Early Childhood.* London: Routledge.

Shute, C. (2002) *Bertrand Russell: 'Education as the Power of Independent Thought'.* Nottingham: Educational Heretics Press.

Smidt, S. (2002) *A Guide to Early Years Practice.* London: Routledge Falmer.

Spodek, B. (1988) 'Conceptualising today's kindergarten curriculum', *The Elementary School Journal,* 89(2): 202–11. www.jstor.org/ (accessed January 2008).

Watson, J.B. (1930) *Behaviourism.* Chicago, IL: University of Chicago Press.

Chapter 2

Andreski, R. and Nicholls, S. (1999) *Managing Your Curriculum: A Practical Guide for Early Years Professionals.* London: Times Supplements.

Aubrey, C. (1997) 'Children's early learning of number in school and out', in I. Thompson (ed.), *Teaching and Learning Early Number.* Maidenhead: Open University/McGraw-Hill Education. pp. 20–9.

Bartlett, S. and Burton, D. (2007) *Introduction to Education Studies.*2nd edn. London: Sage Publications.

Bearne, E. (ed.) (1998) *Use of Language across the Primary Curriculum.* London: Routledge.

Bennett, N., Wood, L. and Rogers, S. (1997) *Teaching Through Play: Teachers' Thinking and Classroom Practice.* Buckingham: Open University Press.

Brown, B. (1998) *Unlearning Discrimination in the Early Years.* Stoke-on-Trent: Trentham Books.

Bruce, T. (2004) *Developing Learning in Early Childhood.* London: Paul Chapman Publishing.

De Boo, M. (2000) *Science 3–6. Laying the Foundations in the Early Years.* Hatfield: Association for Science Education.

Department of Education and Science (DES) (1967) *The Plowden Report.* London: HMSO. www.dg.dial.pipex.com/documents/plowden16.shtml (accessed 17 March 2008).

Department of Education and Science (DES) (1990) *The Rumbold Report: Starting with Quality.* London: HMSO. www.dg.dial.pipex.com/documents/docs1/rumbold01.shtml (accessed 17 March 2008).

Department for Education and Skills (DfES) (2002*) Mathematical Activities for the Foundation Stage: Introductory Pack.* London: Department of Education and Skills.

Department for Education and Skills (DfES) (2007a) *The Statutory Framework for the Early Years Foundation Stage.* London: DfES Publications.

Department for Education and Skills (DfES) (2007b) *Practice Guidance for the Early Years Foundation Stage.* London: Department of Education and Skills.

Drake, J. (2005) *Planning Children's Play and Learning in the Foundation Stage.* 2nd edn. London: David Fulton.

Floyd, A. (1981) *Developing Mathematical Thinking.* London: Addison Wesley/Open University Press.

Gopnik, A., Meltzoff, A. and Kuhl, P. (1999) *How Babies Think.* London: Phoenix.

Griffiths, R. (2005) 'Mathematics and play', in J. Moyles (ed.), *The Excellence of Play.* 2nd edn. Maidenhead: Open University Press.

Liebeck, P. (1984) *How Children Learn Mathematics.* London: Penguin.

Maclellan, E. (1997) 'The importance of counting', in I. Thompson (ed.), *Teaching and Learning Early Number.* Maidenhead: Open University/McGraw-Hill Education. pp. 33–40.

Moyles, J.R. (ed.) (1994) *The Excellence of Play.* Buckingham: Open University Press.

Moyles, J.R. (2005) *The Excellence of Play.* (2nd ed.) Maidenhead: Open University Press.

Munn, P. (1997) 'Children's beliefs about counting', in I. Thompson (ed.), *Teaching and Learning Early Number.* Maidenhead: Open University/McGraw-Hill Education. pp. 9–19.

Qualifications and Curriculum Authority (QCA) (2000) *Curriculum Guidance for the Foundation Stage.* London: QCA. Ch. 1.

Rodger, R. (2003) *Planning an Appropriate Curriculum for the Under Fives; A Guide for Students, Teachers and Assistants.* 2nd edn. London: David Fulton.

Thompson, I. (ed.) (1997) 'The role of counting in derived fact strategies', in I. Thompson (ed.) *Teaching and Learning Early Number*, Maidenhead: Open University/McGraw-Hill Education. pp. 63–72.

Wood, E. and Attfield, J. (2005) *Play, Learning and the Early Childhood Curriculum.* 2nd edn. London: Paul Chapman Publishing.

Wood, L. and Bennett, N. (1997) 'The rhetoric and reality of play: teachers' thinking and classroom practice', *Early Years,* 17(2): 22–7.

Xu, F. and Spelke, E.S. (2000) 'Large number discrimination in 6-month old infants', *Cognition,* 74(1): B1–B11. www.sciencedirect.com/ (accessed May 2008).

Section 2

Chapter 4

Department for Education and Skills (DfES) (2007) *Practice Guidance for the Foundation Stage.* Nottingham: DfES Publications.

Goleman, D. (1995) *Emotional Intelligence: Why It Can Matter More than IQ.* London: Bloomsbury.

Rosenthal, R. and Jacobsen, L. (2003) *Pygmalion in the Classroom.* Crown House.

Chapter 5

Department for Children, Schools and Families (DCSF) (2007) *The Children's Plan: Building Brighter Futures.* Norwich: The Stationery Office.

Department for Education and Skills (DfES) (2007) *The Statutory Framework for the Early Years Foundation Stage.* London: DfES Publications.

Learner, S. (2008) 'Labour pains for Foundation Stage', *Children & Young People Now,* 27 February–4 March: 13.

Office for Standard in Education (OFSTED) (2008) *Quality of Childcare Provision as at 31 December 2007.* London: OFSTED.

Qualifications and Curriculum Authority (QCA) (2003) *Foundation Stage Profile Handbook.* Ref: QCA/03/1006. London: QCA.

Ward, L. (2007) 'Could do better, Ofsted report tells nurseries', *Guardian.* 29 August.

Chapter 6

Abbot, L. and Langston, A. (2004) *Birth to Three Matters: Supporting the Framework for Effective Practice.* Maidenhead: Open University Press.

Bell, J. (2005) *Doing Your Research Project: A Guide for First-Time Researchers in Education, Health and Social Science.* 4th edn. Maidenhead: Open University Press.

Bruce, T. (1997) *Early Childhood Education.* 2nd edn. London: Hodder and Stoughton.

Bruce, T. (2004) *Developing Learning in Early Childhood.* London: Sage Publications.

Claxton, G. and Carr, M. (2004) 'A framework for teaching learning: the dynamics of disposition', *Early Years,* 24(1): 87–97.

Moyles, J. (1989) *Just Playing? The Role and Status of Play in Early Childhood Education.* Buckingham: Open University Press.

Skitton, B. and Fierman, J. (2008) *The Early Years Foundation Stage DIY.* Wocestire: SCA Literacy Training and Development.

Section 3   Introduction

Fabian, H. (2007) 'Crossing borders: the transition to higher education', paper presented at the European Early Childhood Education Research Association 17th Annual Conference, Prague, 29 August–1 September.

Chapter 7

Department for Children, Schools and Families (DCSF) (2008) *Sure Start – Children's Centres.* www.surestart.gov.uk/surestartservices/settings/surestartchildrenscentres/ (accessed 17 February 2008).

Department for Education and Skills (DfES) (1998) *Sure Start the 1998 Green Paper.* www.surestart.gov.uk/aboutsurestart/about/thesurestartprogramme2/challenge/ (accessed 28 April 2008).

McAuliffe, A.-M., Linsey, A. and Fowler, J. (2006) *Childcare Act 2006: The Essential Guide.* London: NFER and NCB.

O'Toole, J. (1996) *Leading Change – The Argument for Value-Based Leadership.* New York: Ballantine Books.

Chapter 8

Aubrey, C. (2007) *Leading and Managing in the Early Years*. London: Sage Publications.

Elsevier (2005) *Management Extra. Leading Teams*. Oxford: Elsevier/Butterworth-Heinemann.

Moyles, J. (2006) *Effective Leadership and Management in the Early Years*. Maidenhead: Open University Press.

Tuckman, B. (1965) *Forming, Storming, Norming, Performing Team Development Model*. www.business
balls.com (accessed 19 March 2008).

Chapter 9

Anning, A., Cottrell, D., Frost, N., Green, J. and Robinson, M. (2006) *Developing Multiprofessional Teamwork for Integrated Children's Services*. Maidenhead: Open University Press.

Department for Children, Schools and Families (DCSF) (2007a) *The Children's Plan: Building Brighter Futures*. Norwich: Stationery Office.

Department for Children, Schools and Families (DCSF) (2007b) *Effective Integrated Working: Findings of the Concept of Operations Study*. London: The Stationery Office.

Department for Education and Employment (DfEE) (1999) *Building on Success*, Green Paper. London: The Stationery Office.

Department for Education and Skills, Department of Health and Home Office (2003) *Keeping Children Safe: The Government's Response to the Victoria Climbié Inquiry Report and Chief Inspector's Report Safeguarding Children*. London: The Stationery Office.

Frost, N. (2005) *Professionalism, Partnership and Joined Up Thinking*. Dartington: Research in Practice.

Hermajesty's Triasury (2005) *Every Child Matters*. Green paper. London: The Stationary Office.

Shaw, P. (2006) *The Four Vs of Leadership; Vision, Values, Value Added, Vitality*. Chichester: Capstone.

Section 4

Chapter 10

Adair, J. (2003) *The Inspirational Leader*. London: Kogan Page.

Egolf, D. (2001) *Forming, Storming, Norming, Performing: Successful Communication in Groups and Teams*. Lincoln, NE: Writers Club Press.

Blanchard, K. (2007) *Leading at a Higher Level*. London: Prentice Hall.

Thomas, N. (2003) *Adair on Leadership*. London: Thorogood Publishing.

Tuckman, B. (1965) *Forming, Storming, Norming, Performing Team Development Model*. www.business
batts.com (accessed 31 March 2008).

Chapter 11

Baumrind, D. (1972) 'Socialisation and Instrumental competence in young children'. In W.W.Hartrup (ed.), *The Young Child: review of research* (Vol 2) Washington, DC: National Association for the Education of Young Children.

Bruce, T. (2005) *Learning Through Play: Babies, Toddlers and the Foundation Years.* London: Hodder and Stoughton.

Daly, M., Byers, E. and Taylor, W. (2004) *Early Years Management in Practice.* Oxford: Heinemann.

Department for Children Education and Lifelong Learning Skills (DCELLS) (2007) *Foundation Phase National Training Pack.* Cardiff: Welsh Assembly Government.

Fabian, H. (2002) *Children Starting School.* London: David Fulton.

Gordon, A.M. and Browne, K.W. (2000) *Beginnings and Beyond.* 5th edn. Albany, NY: Delmar.

Harrison, R., Mann, G., Murphy, M., Taylor, A. and Thompson, N. (2003) *Partnership Made Painless.* Lyme Regis: Russell House.

Home-Start UK (2003) *Could You Help Us Make a Difference for Families?* Leicester: Home-Start.

Lindon, J. and Lindon, L. (1997) *Working Together for Young Children.* Basingstoke: Macmillan.

Lord Laming (2003) The Victoria Climbié Inquiry: report of an inquiry by Lord Laming. Norwich: HMSO.

Marrow, G. and Malin, N. (2004) 'Parents and professionals working together', *Early Years an International Journal of Research and Development,* 24(2): 163–77.

May, P. and Nurse, A.D. (2007) 'Birth to three', in A.D. Nurse (ed.), *The New Early Years Professional: Dilemmas and Debates.* London: Routledge.

Miller, L., Cable, C. and Devereux, J. (2005) *Developing Early Years Practice.* London: David Fulton.

Oates, J. (ed.) (1994) *The Foundations of Child Development.* Oxford: Blackwell.

Panksepp, J. (1998) *Affective Neuroscience. The Foundations of Human and Animal Emotions.* Oxford: Oxford University Press.

Rogers, C. (2003) *Client Centred Therapy.* London: Constable.

Sunderland, M. (2004) *Helping Children with Low Self-Esteem.* Oxford: Speechmark.

Sunderland, M. (2005) *Helping Children Who Yearn for Someone They Love.* Oxford: Speechmark.

Chapter 12

Bowlby, J. (1965) *Child Care and the Growth of Love.* 2nd edn. London: Pelican

Department for Education and Skills (DfES) (2002) *Birth to Three Matters.* London: DfES Publications.

Gopnik, A., Meltzoff, M. and Kuhl, P. (2001) *How Babies Think.* London: Phoenix.

Meggitt, C. (2006) *Child Development An Illustrated Guide.* Oxford: Heinemann.

Sharp, P. (2001) *Nurturing Emotional Literacy.* London: David Fulton.

Conclusion

Effective Provision of Pre-School Education (EPPE) project. www.ioe.ac.uk/schools/ecpe/eppe/ (accessed 31 March 08).

Gonzalez, T. (2007) 'Promoting learning and development in the early years through play', *Early Childhood Matters,* November (109).

Tuckman, B. (1965) *Forming, Storming, Norming, Performing Team Development Model.* www.business balls.com (accessed 31 March 2008).

Index

Added to a page number 'f' denotes a figure and 't' denotes a table.